Introduction to Mechanical System Simulation Using Adams

Author:

James B. McConville
Technical Fellow
MSC Software Corporation
Ann Arbor, MI

Publications

SDC Publications
P.O. Box 1334
Mission, KS 66222
913-262-2664
www.SDCpublications.com
Publisher: Stephen Schroff

ISBN-13: 978-1-58503-988-3
ISBN-10: 1-58503-988-8

Printed and bound in the United States of America.

Obtaining Supplemental Files

Please visit www.mscsoftware.com/adamstextbook to download the exercise problems. On this page, we also provide a link to the **Adams Curriculum Kit**, which contains 44 additional exercise problems to help you get started with the software.

Alternatively, the exercise files can be downloaded from
www.SDCpublications.com/downloads/978-1-58503-988-3

Contents

Dedication

To: Nicki Orlandea for his brilliance in laying the theoretical foundations of Adams

To: Mike Korybalski for his entrepreneurial acumen and great generosity, both of which he demonstrated in ample measure when bringing Adams to Market

J.B. McConville
Ann Arbor
2015

About the Author

Jim has a Bachelor's degree in Aerospace Engineering from the University of Virginia, and a Master's Degree in Language Education from the University of Georgia where he studied German and Russian. Jim has had numerous career achievements and held impressive positions including Aircraft Structures Engineer at Lockheed; Design Engineer of underground coal mining equipment at Lee-Norse, subsidiary of Ingersoll Rand; Design Engineer of material handling equipment at Clark Equipment Company; and Consulting Engineer at Mechanical Dynamics Inc. (MDI), acquired in 2002 by MSC Software. Jim was also awarded the ranking of Technical Fellow at MSC Software for his contributions to Computer Aided Engineering (CAE). Jim has pioneered many of the modeling techniques used by engineers today in combining finite element analysis and multibody dynamics to solve previously insoluble problems. He was one of the first to recognize the potential of multibody dynamics in the aerospace, machinery, defense and consumer goods industries, and has guided the analytical approach to many commercial projects. Jim's hobbies include Rugby football and aviation history.

Introduction

The Significance of Large Motion

Multibody Dynamics (hereafter referred to using the acronym MBD) is typified most of all by its ability to efficiently deal with appreciable motion. Such motion, and especially rotational motion, tends to be highly non-linear in the spatial sense. Compounding this are effects which vary non-linearly with time. Thus, all aspects of an MBD problem are usually mathematically very non-linear. This is where Adams shines. It is specifically designed to deal efficiently with these nonlinearities. However, there is a price to be paid for this capability. A reader who is familiar with Finite Element Analysis (FEA) may be used to dealing with structural systems possessing hundreds of thousands of points of interest (e.g., "nodes" or "grids"), perhaps even millions of such points. While such models are extremely valuable, they are very often limited by the assumption of linearity if they are to remain computationally tractable. In other words, the assumption is made that the motion of all the points of interest is so limited that it doesn't have to be tracked during the analysis, and the starting point positions are all that is needed. As we shall see later in this book, that is a serious restriction on what kinds of analysis can validly be performed. Because it is basic to the Adams MBD approach, the motion of the points of interest **must** be tracked, which limits the number of points of interest which can be considered if the Adams analysis is to remain tractable. As we shall see, however, there are methods which permit the direct use of linear FEA structures in Adams MBD models. Currently, extension of the Adams MBD capability to include complex structural nonlinearity is accomplished using co-simulation methods, which are beyond the scope of this book. Methods to efficiently include structural non-linearity directly in Adams, without resort to co-simulation, are under development as this book is published.

The Intent and Scope of This Book

This book is intended to familiarize the reader with the basics of theory and practice in Adams MBD modeling. The content has been developed to be beneficial to readers who are students or practicing engineers who are either completely new to MBD modeling or have some experience with MBD modeling. While this book is neither software user documentation nor a training guide, the author's lengthy experience using the Adams software adds a practical and, occasionally, humorous complement to standard documentation and training materials, intended to benefit the reader learning Adams. The book features relatively small examples which can be readily built and executed by the reader. This book contains an introduction to Adams theory which provides the basics on how Adams models are formulated and then numerically solved. These sections are deliberately limited and make no claim to comprehensiveness. Finally, this book concludes with some "success stories" taken from industry.

Acknowledgements

The Adams (**A**utomatic **D**ynamic **A**nalysis of **M**echanical **S**ystems) program has its origins in the brilliant PhD thesis written at the University of Michigan in 1973 by Dr. Nicolae Orlandea (reference [5]). Using this thesis as a foundation, 3 University of Michigan pioneering software entrepreneurs (Dr. Milt Chace, Mike Korybalski, and John Angell) founded Mechanical Dynamics, Inc. (MDI) in 1976. The rest is history.

The author would also like to thank Dr. Frank Owen and Dr. Xi Wu, both of Cal Poly, for their critiques and assistance in generating this book. Further thanks go also to Leslie Bodnar of MSC for getting the ball rolling and to John Janevic of MSC for his skill and perseverance in editing the text. Finally, a *very* special thanks is due to Dominic Gallello, President and CEO of MSC Software, without whose vision, inspiration, encouragement, and support this book would not have happened.

An Example to Come

The figure below gives the reader a brief foretaste of the kind of analyses possible with Adams MBD analysis. The backhoe excavator shown is one of the sample problems examined in great detail later in this book.

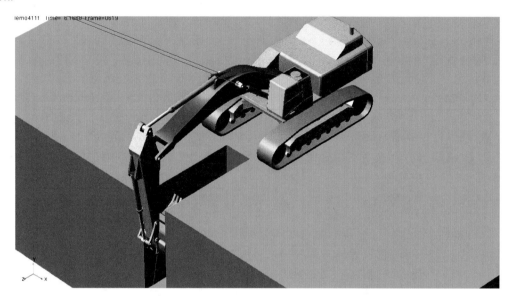

Figure 1 Excavator with Flexible Boom Arm Performing a Typical Duty Cycle

The reader will be shown how to represent articulating Adams parts defined by CAD geometry, how to connect and drive those parts so that the system moves correctly, how to load the system appropriately, and how to interrogate the model for results. Finally, the excavator boom, initially modeled as a rigid body, will be rendered flexible using MSC Nastran, and the effects of its flexibility on the modeling results will be demonstrated.

A brief note on conventions used throughout the examples and text in this book: capital letters (e.g. "PART") are generally used to denote keywords and parameters in the Adams or MSC Nastran modeling languages; however, in practice capitalization is not necessary for these keywords and parameters. Every attempt is made to relate keywords to common terminology (e.g. "CBAR" is a beam element in the MSC Nastran modeling language), but where this has been missed or insufficiently explained, the reader is invited to refer to Adams and/or MSC Nastran documentation (details in the References section).

Finally, at various points in the book, it will be helpful if the reader has some familiarity with the traditional usage paradigm of MBD (and FEA) tools:

- The user builds models of the product to be analyzed in a "preprocessor" or "user interface" (e.g. Adams/View or Patran)
- The preprocessor generates a representation of the product and its relevant mechanical characteristics in the native modeling language of the "solver" (e.g. Adams or MSC Nastran)
- Input to the solver consists of the model definition as well as a set of instructions for what analysis to perform
- The solver generates and numerically solves the appropriate equations, generating (often large) amounts of numerical output
- The user will then load the numerical output files into the "postprocessor" (e.g. Adams/View or Patran) for convenience in interpreting the results (animations, plots, etc.)

MSC is at the forefront of innovations to this traditional usage paradigm as the steps in FEA and MBD become highly interactive, with exciting developments to come.

Elementary Adams Theory

Basic Formulations

As commented on in the introduction, there are some fundamental differences between the FEA (Finite Element Analysis) and MBD (Multibody Dynamics) approaches to the analysis of an articulating mechanical system. In this theory section, the basic contrasts between the two approaches will be examined initially. Subsequently, a pendulum example will be dissected in some detail, with the intent being to show the basics of MBD equation formulation and subsequent numerical solution.

The MBD Approach

Based on the principles of Lagrangian Dynamics, Adams numerically constructs and solves the system equations as functions of time. These equations are usually both algebraic and differential as well as highly nonlinear. The basic approach employed by Adams uses Lagrange's formulation of the 2nd form:

$$1) \quad \mathbf{F}_j = \frac{d}{dt}\left(\frac{\partial L}{\partial \dot{\mathbf{q}}_j}\right) - \frac{\partial L}{\partial \mathbf{q}_j} + \sum_{i=1}^{m}\frac{\partial \Phi_q^{\mathrm{T}}}{\partial \mathbf{q}_j}\lambda_i - \mathbf{Q}_j = 0 \qquad \text{for } j = 1, \dots n$$

$$2) \quad \Phi_i = 0$$

Where:

$\mathbf{q}$	= generalized coordinate
F	= the equilibrium equation in the direction of generalized coordinate q
L	= the Lagrangian (T-V) where T → kinetic energy; V → potential energy
Φ	= algebraic constraint equations
λ	= Lagrange multiplier
$\mathbf{Q}$	= generalized Force
n	= # of generalized coordinates
m	= # of constraint equations (< or = n)

In the general case, the Q's can be functions of q and time. The Φ's are either constant (scleronomic) or continuous, time-varying (holonomic) algebraic constraints. In general, the Adams solution is *always* iterative. If $m = n$, all motion is pre-determined (i.e., the system has zero Degrees of Freedom, or "DOFs"), and the constraint equations alone are adequate to solve the problem, with any resulting forces being back-calculated. If the problem is time-invariant, but n is greater than m, the solution, if feasible, is an iterated, quasi-static result with time-invariant Q's playing a role in the solution.

The FEA Approach

The FEA equations are Newtonian in form and employ coordinates which are spatially orthogonal

$$3) \quad \{\mathbf{F}\} = [\mathbf{M}]\{\ddot{\mathbf{x}}\} + [\mathbf{C}]\{\dot{\mathbf{x}}\} + [\mathbf{K}]\{\mathbf{x}\}$$

Where:

x	= coordinate
F	= the equilibrium forces in the orthogonal (Cartesian) coordinates
M	= the mass matrix
C	= the damping matrix
K	= the stiffness matrix

In the general case, F, M, C, and K can be functions of x and time. In the simplest case, when x is time invariant, K is constant, and the problem is not otherwise ill-posed, equation 3 submits to a single step solution.

If the problem at hand is linear, both the FEA and MBD methods can produce valid, frequency domain solutions. If equation 3 is time-invariant and the coefficient matrices are constant, an eigenvalue solution is directly obtainable. In Adams, equation set 1 must first be linearized about some bona fide equilibrium point.

In what follows, the frequency domain will not be further considered, and attention will be limited to time-varying, dynamic solutions only. Suffice it to say that "Physics is Physics" and, to be correct, both FEA and MBD must give the same results when applied to the same engineering problem. The deciding factor as to which method is employed must be based on which solution is most tractable and practical.

Elementary Overview of Solution Approaches

FEA Transient Response Analysis – Explicit Integration

The direct transient response analysis in MSC Nastran (known in shorthand as "SOLUTION 109" or "SOL109") is typical of the MSC Nastran FEA time-domain approach to the FEA solution of dynamical problems (for a more detailed description of the MSC Nastran approach, the reader is directed to reference [2]). In brief, the equations are solved using a modified Newmark-Beta approach. In its most efficient form, the time step size is fixed, and the coefficient matrices in equation 3 are constant. The instantaneous velocities and accelerations are derived from central divided differences which divide consecutive displacements by the time step for velocities and divide consecutive displacements by the square of the time step for accelerations. In effect, this converts the problem into a pseudo-static form at each new point in time, permitting the use of standard matrix inversion coding. This solution is

explicit, meaning that each advance in time is determined from past, converged time steps only. This has important implications, as will be discussed in the examples to follow.

MBD Transient Response Analysis – Implicit Integration

Adams has several different solvers, including an explicit one similar to that employed by MSC Nastran SOL700. It is seldom used. Instead, implicit solvers, which use predicted states to advance in time, are employed. The use of implicit predictor-corrector solvers has profound implications for the solution of a broad class of dynamical problems.

To illustrate the Adams implicit solution approach, let us postulate a very simple, unconstrained dynamics problem in a single generalized coordinate **q**. The Adams equation set (equations 1 & 2) reduces to:

$$4) \quad \mathbf{F} = \mathbf{Q} - \mathbf{f(q)} = \mathbf{E} \Rightarrow \mathbf{0}$$

Where:

f(q)   = some nonlinear function of **q**
E   = equilibrium error (to be driven to zero)

Fig. 2 shows the initial prediction forward in time.

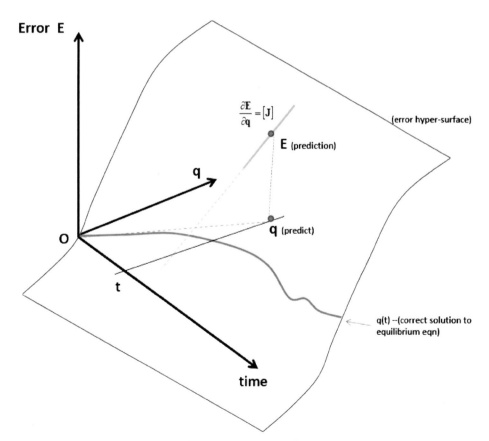

Figure 2 Predictor-Corrector Solution Space

The initial predictor equation is 1st order and uses a default time step to advance the solution to time *t*. The predicted value of **q** will, in general, not satisfy the equilibrium equation and will result in an error **E**. With time fixed at *t*, the equation set is numerically differenced around the predicted **q** to determine the error change with **q**. This determines the tangent to the *n*-dimensional error hyper-plane. This is called the Jacobian **[J]**. Note that, in our simplified example, *n*=1 and the Jacobian is a simple tangent line to the error hyper-surface at **q**. In general, *n* will be much larger than 1, and the Jacobian will be an n-dimensional, osculating hyper-plane to the *n*-dimensional error hyper-surface (just try to draw that on a 2-D piece of paper!).

Since the predicted solution results in error, it must be modified, if it can be, to reduce the error to within the requested error tolerance. To accomplish this, modified Newton-Raphson iteration is employed. The corrections to the predicted **q** are determined from:

5) $\quad \mathbf{E} + \left[\dfrac{\partial \mathbf{E}}{\partial \mathbf{q}} \right] \Delta \mathbf{q} = \mathbf{E} + [\mathbf{J}]\Delta \mathbf{q} = \mathbf{0}$

6) $\quad \Delta \mathbf{q} = -[\mathbf{J}]^{-1}\mathbf{E}$

This process is repeated as shown schematically in Fig. 3.

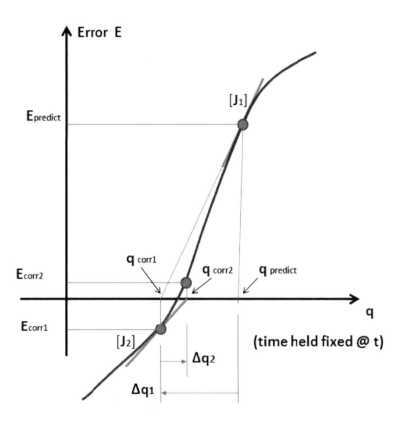

Figure 3 Newton-Raphson Iteration

If the error criterion cannot be met, the time step is reduced, and the process is repeated. Even if the corrector converges, the change in **q** must satisfy the remainder limit of the Taylor series expansion of the predicting polynomial. If this criterion is not met, the converged time step is discarded, the integrator "back-steps" in time, returning to the previously-converged time step (or back to the starting initial conditions if the analysis is just beginning), and starts the process again with a less aggressive predictor time step.

As the time solution progresses, more converged history is available for all the **q**'s, and, in order to minimize solution time, the solver will try, based on numerical criteria, to increase the time step size (the output step size is the upper limit) and will also try to increase the order of the predicting polynomial (maximum order used in Adams is 6).

The term "modified" is applied to the iteration scheme because, to speed the solution, it is not always necessary to update the system Jacobian at each iteration. A major computational cost in Adams is associated with the computation of the Jacobian inverse. For this reason the inverse of the Jacobian is "mapped" so that it can be quickly updated. Further, the inverse selected is a compromise chosen between maintenance of system equation set sparsity and retention of adequate equation set numerical conditioning. Sparsity is critical to fast solution speed, and system matrices that are only 3-5% populated are not uncommon. However, if upon updating during the solution, the Jacobian should sufficiently degrade (one or more of the terms being used as pivot for solution purposes approaches zero), it is "re-factorized" (e.g. re-mapped) and new pivots are chosen to restore equation set health. Problems which continually re-factorize are generally poorly defined and/or ill-posed.

Numerical "Stiffness"

A numerically "stiff" system is one possessing widely split eigenvalues. Fig. 4 depicts a 2 DOF spring/mass/damper system in which the masses are constrained to move vertically. Assume that **K1** and **C1** are large, that **K2** and **C2** are small, and that the resulting undamped system eigenfrequencies are 5 kHz and 5 Hz. Assume further that at least 10 output steps are necessary to track a complete

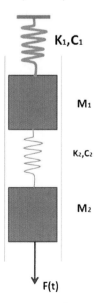

Figure 4 Excited 2 DOF Spring/Mass/Damper System

deformation cycle. This implies that the maximum permissible time step is 2.0e-5 seconds as long as the 5 kHz motion is present. An explicit solver always assumes the highest potential frequency in the system may be active, thus the integrator step is "maxed" at 2.0e-5. An implicit integrator, on the other hand, "senses" the highest, *currently-active* system frequency and opens the time stepping accordingly. Assume for the moment that **F(t)** initially excites the 5 kHz motion but that the damping factor **C₁** quickly drives this motion to zero. The implicit solver can now, since it is now dealing with a 5 Hz problem, increase the step size to 2.0e-2 second, resulting in a thousand-fold improvement in execution speed, and the time step will stay there unless *F(t)* should, again, excite the high frequency. Even if *F(t)* is not a source of high frequency excitation, the numerical solution itself of the system equations can result in solver "noise," leading to spurious system frequency excitation. This points out the importance of *always* including damping, however small it may be, in a simulation. It is always present when materials dynamically deform, except, perhaps, for those esoteric cases where the temperature of the deforming material approaches absolute zero.

There are potential issues with use of an implicit solver. A successful (i.e., converging) explicit solution will, in general, also be numerically accurate. A converging implicit solution may not be, unless the error control is sufficiently tight. A "rule of thumb" associated with implicit solvers is that the solution is not truly accurate unless the results stop changing with successive reductions in error tolerance. This consideration is often overlooked in practice.

In addition to MSC Nastran SOL109, other capabilities in the MSC Nastran FEA solution suite are SOLUTION 400 (implicit nonlinear analysis, based on MSC's Marc solver) and SOLUTION 700 (explicit nonlinear analysis, based on LSTC's LS-DYNA solver). SOL700 is limited to explicit numerical solution. MSC Nastran SOL109 and SOL400, like Adams, solve implicitly (at least by preference). The decision as to which solution to employ depends in large part on the importance of certain problem attributes.

Problem Attributes

The decision as to which solution to employ for an engineering problem depends on, in addition to explicit/implicit solver considerations, other factors, some principle ones of which are:

1) Constitutive Considerations
2) Degree-of-Freedom (DOF) Count – Structural vs. Mechanism
3) Event Motion/ Duration

Constitutive Considerations – Deformable vs. Non-Deformable

Rigid Components

If the structural deformation of the system components can be ignored (i.e., the components are considered rigid), MBD is the automatic choice. Even if the connections between the components are functionally complex, FEA cannot hope to compete in computational efficiency, completeness, and ease of use. MBD, with its algebraic constraint capability and its use of convecting reference frames (see below) is specifically designed to deal very efficiently with this type of problem.

Hookean Components

If the structural deformation of the system components is linear – deformations are small and the material is linearly elastic (e.g., Hookean)—the FEA/MBD selection decision generally depends on whether the system contains mechanism freedoms. If it does, and especially if the components undergo large rigid-body motions, an MBD model employing modally-reduced, MSC Nastran generated, linear FEA substructures, whose properties have been captured in an MNF (Modal Neutral File) is almost certainly the most viable approach.[1]

If the system is linear, contiguous, and non-mechanistic, but subjected to non-steady-state excitation (a problem somewhat limited in scope), a dynamic transient approach in MSC Nastran (SOL109) might be viable and preferred.

Non-Hookean Components

If a system component is non-Hookean (say, non-linear elastic or elasto-plastic), the constitutive equations must become functions of time as well as position, and direct application of SOL109 becomes impractical. While Adams theoretically permits the definition of any kind of non-linear structural elements as forces or general state equations (GSEs), the prodigious effort involved in their implementation effectively precludes their consideration. For problems involving non-linear material behavior, consideration should be limited to MSC Nastran's implicit and explicit solution capabilities (SOL400 and SOL700).

Special Case – Non-Linear, Body-to-Body Contact

If system components can come into contact, MBD is preferred on computational grounds if the components are rigid or linearly elastic and the Hertzian nature of the contact (localized forces and deformation) is of less importance than the gross deformation of the contacting bodies. Such contact effects do not violate the linearity restriction associated with the Adams flexible part because they are applied to the boundary (i.e., the *exterior*) of the component. As long as the gross deformations remain linear and the contact meshing is reasonable, the results will be valid.

If the Hertzian effects are paramount or non-Hookean effects are in play, SOL400 and SOL700 are to be preferred.

DOF Count

In broad terms, the FEA approach is ideal for dealing with components possessing a very large number of points (called GRIDs in MSC Nastran parlance) undergoing (preferably) small displacements from the un-loaded state. If the displacements are negligible with respect to the system dimensions and permit the use of the un-deformed point coordinates for all time – an enormous computational cost savings results.

MBD, on the other hand, is ideal for dealing with the complex, generally non-linear, motion of a relatively small number of points (called MARKERs in Adams parlance).

---

[1] **Caveat**: If any of the system components experience large spin velocities, stress-stiffening effects may become important, but these will not be captured by the linear MNF. Special modeling methods which exploit the MBD convecting reference frame capability may be required (see below).

Important to these concepts are the differences between global and convecting reference frames.

System Motion (Global vs. Convecting Reference Frames)

FEA computes all point (i.e. GRID) positions with respect to a grounded reference frame (refer to figure 5). Even if a moving component is unloaded in the Newtonian sense (say, translating at constant velocity but not rotating), FEA requires the re-computation of all point locations and the re-formulation of all constitutive equations at every solution step.

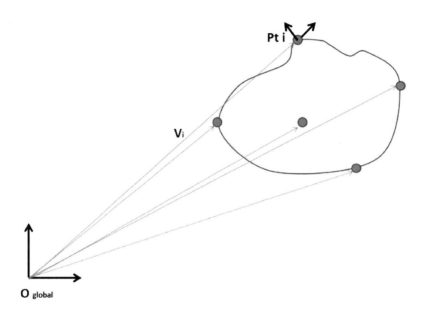

Figure 5 FEA Location Tracking—All Points Referenced to Global Origin

For each component in an MBD model (figure 6), there is an associated Local Part Reference Frame (LPRF). For a rigid part, the global point positions are determined by tracking the LPRF translation and rotation with respect to ground and using the **QG** vector and the LPRF Euler angles **{EU}** transformations to operate on the (unchanging) **QP** vectors to determine the global position components of the points (i.e., the q's from equation 1). If the part in question is flexible, the LPRF is located at the origin of the FEA model used to create it, and the (linear) LPRF-referenced point deflections, determined from equilibrium conditions of equation 1, are added to the **QP** vectors for transformation to global.

16

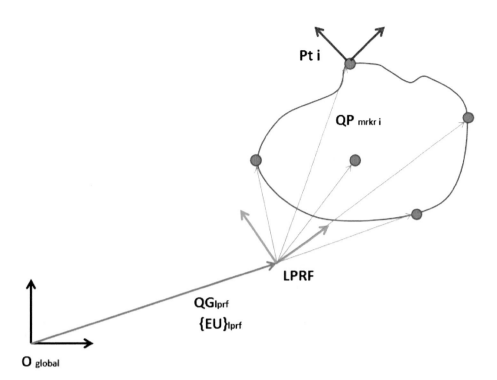

Figure 6 MBD Location Tracking – Body Points Referenced to LPRF and LPRF to Global Origin

It must be remembered that the number of points which is typically tracked in an MBD solution is very small compared to what is traditional in FEA. That said, when an FEA solution must deal with large motions and/or non-Hookean material effects, the solution times for even small problems (say, on the order of 1e4 DOF) can become prohibitive.

Large (Nonlinear but Still Hookean) Geometric Effects

Figure 7 below shows 2 versions of the same simple cantilever beam. The MSC Nastran FEA model consists of 3 evenly-spaced GRIDs, 2 beam elements (CBARs), 6 single point constraints (SPCs) on GRID 1, and 1 applied force (FORCE) entry on GRID 3. The applied force is a non-follower applied in the global Y-direction. When run as a single-step, linear static (SOL101) solution in MSC Nastran, the linear, transverse deflection limit applies and the transverse deflection of the beam tip cannot exceed 10% of the total beam length. Further, the beam exhibits no foreshortening, and the X-positions of GRIDs 2 & 3 remain unchanged.

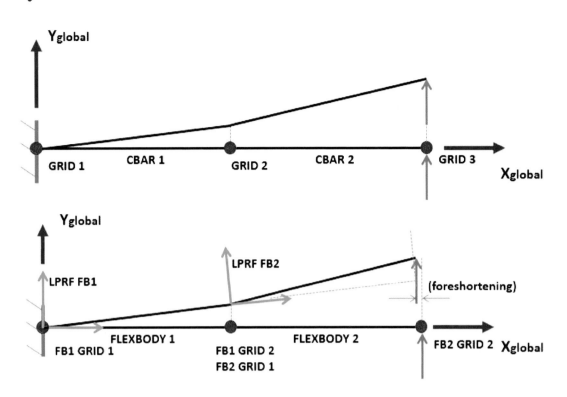

Figure 7 Simple Beam Model -- Linear FEA (Top) vs. MBD (Bottom)

The Adams MBD model uses the same basic elements and geometry as the FEA model to generate a flexible part (known as a "FLEXBODY" in Adams). FLEXBODY 1 consists of the CBAR spanning GRIDs 1 & 2 rendered as an FEA superelement using MSC Nastran modal condensation analysis (in SOL103). FLEXBODY 2 can be separately generated from a separate SOL103 analysis using GRID locations 2 & 3, or, as is done here for simplicity, FLEXBODY 1 can simply be copied and translated to create FB2. One 6-DOF fixed joint anchors FB1 GRID 1 to ground and another affixes FB2 GRID 1 to FB1 GRID 2. The load is applied at FB2 GRID 2. It must be emphasized that the MBD FLEXBODYs are structurally *identical* to the FEA CBAR elements and conform to the same limitations of the Euler-Timoshenko beam formulation. When loaded, just as with the FEA model, FLEXBODY 1 does not foreshorten with respect to its LPRF, which is coincident with the global reference frame. Nor, of course, does FLEXBODY 2 foreshorten with respect to its LPRF, ***but, the FB2 LPRF has moved – CONVECTED – with respect to the global reference frame. As a result, even though the beam (linear) constitutive equations are unchanged (i.e., are constant and un-iterated), geometrically-based, non-linear structural foreshortening has been introduced into the solution!*** In addition, while each FLEXBODY is still individually subject to the 10% limit on transverse tip deflection, the MBD model permits greater assembly tip travel before one of the FLEXBODYs reaches its individual limit. The more FLEXBODYs that are employed for a given beam length, the further the tip can be displaced. The results will be valid until the 10% rule is locally violated by one of the FLEXBODYs or until the material strain within one of the FLEXBODYs exceeds the Hookean limit.

For beam structures, 2 FLEXBODYs are the minimum number needed to initiate the capture of foreshortening effects. Most practical (beam-like) applications need no more than 5 FLEXBODYs to produce very accurate, large-displacement results. In addition to foreshortening, other non-linear

effects such as the inertial stress-stiffening of spun systems can be effectively captured using multiple, convecting, structurally linear FLEXBODYs.

The MBD method described above can be extended to beam-like structures comprised of 2D shell or 3D solid elements, but the number of substructure re-connection points must be kept small, which implies the use of surrogate elements (e.g., MSC Nastran RBE elements) to reduce the number of re-connection points at the substructure interfaces. However, this can undesirably effect the substructure stiffnesses. Efforts to evolve methods to ameliorate this effect are currently under way at MSC.

It is, perhaps, useful to contrast the FEA and MBD approaches in a summary table. This is attempted below.

Aspect	FEA (Newtonian)	Adams MBD (Lagrangian)	Remarks
Formulational Basis	equilibrium	energy	
Orthogonality	spatial	mathematical	
Dimensionality	2D/3D	3D	
Location Reference	global	Local and global	MSA employs "convecting" reference frames
Rigid Components	possible	standard	
Flexible Components	standard	limited	In Adams, complex structures limited to linear (modal) representation
DOF Count	Almost unlimited	limited	
Equation Processing	1 step or iterated	iterated	
Solver Types	Usually explicit	Usually implicit	
Solution Domain	Frequency/time	Predominantly Time	Adams Vibration permits solution in the frequency domain
Solution Duration	Potentially enormous	Usually modest	

Table 1 – Summary Contrasting FEA and MBD Approaches

The Pendulum in Theory

A simple pendulum serves as a very useful tool by which to gain a feeling for the basic Adams formulation. It is small enough to be tractable, yet complete enough to be informative. The theoretical pendulum analyses that follow are taken directly from [1]. Note that, while Adams is intrinsically a 3-dimensional code, the sample pendulum equations will, for sake of brevity, be developed in 2-dimensional (i.e., planar) space.

The figure on the next page illustrates the geometry of a simple, single degree-of-freedom pendulum.

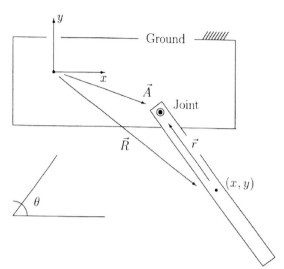

Figure 8 Simple, Planar, 1 DOF Pendulum

In figure 8:

1) The pendulum body possesses a mass of **m** and a mass moment of inertia of **I.**
2) The XY axes locate and orient the global origin (i.e., the Newtonian reference frame).
3) **A** is the fixed (i.e., *constant*), global vector which locates the pendulum hinge center.
4) **R** is the variable position vector from the ground origin to the pendulum body mass center.
5) The doublet (x,y) locates the instantaneous, global position of the pendulum body CG.
6) **r** is pendulum body-fixed, *constant* vector from the pendulum body CG to the pendulum hinge. Note that this vector is variable when expressed in global coordinates.
7) **Θ** shows the positive sense of angular rotation.
8) Gravity (not shown) acts in the global negative y-direction.

Comment: like all, classical physics problems obeying Newton's laws, the system equations must be expressed in a non-accelerating, *inertial* reference frame. Thus, "ground" in the figure represents the "center of the Universe" for the model. As a practical matter, for most applications, ground can be Earth-fixed, although it should not be forgotten that this neglects Coriolis effects, which may be important for some problems, such as the behavior of orbiting spacecraft and ballistics.

Formulating the System Equations

Energy Terms and the Lagrangian

The entire kinetic energy of this system is contained in the pendulum body and is given by:

$$7) \quad T = \frac{1}{2}\left(m\dot{x}^2 + m\dot{y}^2 + I\dot{\theta}^2\right)$$

Similarly, the entire potential energy of the system can be expressed as:

$$8) \quad V = mgy$$

The Lagrangian can be written as:

$$9) \quad L = T - V$$

If there were more bodies in the system, the Lagrangian would have to include their energy terms as well.

Repeating equation 1 but simplifying it to represent our system with its single moving part:

$$10) \quad \frac{d}{dt}\left(\frac{\partial L}{\partial \dot{q}}\right) - \frac{\partial L}{\partial q} + \Phi_q^T \lambda = Q$$

For those more used to Newtonian mechanics, equation 10 can seem somewhat impenetrable and in need of further explanation. Generating these terms for the pendulum model, one arrives at:

...the generalized coordinates for the system are;

11)

$$q = \left\{ \begin{matrix} x \\ y \\ \theta \end{matrix} \right\}$$

...and, since the Lagrangian is a scalar and q is an array;

12)

$$\frac{\partial L}{\partial q} = \left\{ \begin{matrix} \dfrac{\partial L}{\partial q_1} \\ \dfrac{\partial L}{\partial q_2} \\ * \\ * \\ * \\ \dfrac{\partial L}{\partial q_n} \end{matrix} \right\}$$

Equation 12 represents, in effect, the sensitivity of the Lagrangian to each of the system's generalized coordinates.

Similarly, the sensitivity of the Lagrangian to the time derivatives of the generalized coordinates is given by:

13)

$$\frac{\partial L}{\partial \dot{q}} = \left\{ \begin{matrix} \dfrac{\partial L}{\partial \dot{q}_1} \\ \dfrac{\partial L}{\partial \dot{q}_2} \\ * \\ * \\ * \\ \dfrac{\partial L}{\partial \dot{q}_n} \end{matrix} \right\}$$

Equation 13 represents, in effect, the sensitivity of the Lagrangian to each of the system's generalized velocities.

The (algebraic) constraint effects are brought into play with...

14)

$$\Phi_q = \frac{\partial \Phi}{\partial q}$$

Equation 14 defines the constraint Jacobian. It is an n by m rectangular array, with n being the number of generalized coordinates and m being the number of applied constraints.

In summary, and referring to equation 10:

1) The term Φ_q^T is the n by m rectangular array which couples the constraints into the force-equilibrium equations (where m is the number of constraint conditions, n is the number of generalized coordinates, and superscript T denotes the transpose).
2) The column matrix Q contains the externally-applied, non-potential forces in the model
3) The term $\frac{d}{dt}\left(\frac{\partial L}{\partial \dot{q}}\right)$ represents the accelerations of the mechanical components
4) The term $\frac{\partial L}{\partial q}$ contains the potential forces (e.g., gravitational forces in our pendulum model)
5) The term $\Phi_q^T \lambda$ supplies the constraint forces where λ is the column matrix of the $m < n$ (algebraic) Lagrange multipliers

Using the definitions in equations 7 and 9, a review of the term $\left(\frac{\partial L}{\partial \dot{q}}\right)$ reveals that it is simply the system momentum associated with the generalized coordinate q. Thus:

15)

$$p_{q=}\frac{\partial L}{\partial \dot{q}}$$

If q is either of the translational coordinates (x or y) of our pendulum mass center, the time derivative of equation 15 yields:

16)

$$\frac{d}{dt}\left(\frac{\partial L}{\partial \dot{q}}\right) = \dot{p}_q = m\ddot{q}$$

If q is the rotational coordinate θ of our pendulum mass center, the time derivative of equation 15 yields:

17)

$$\frac{d}{dt}\left(\frac{\partial L}{\partial \dot{q}}\right) = \dot{p}_q = I\ddot{q}$$

The three coordinates associated with the pendulum body are x, y, and θ. Populating the Lagrangian-related terms in equation 10 with these terms:

18)

$$\frac{d}{dt}\left(\frac{\partial L}{\partial \dot{q}}\right) - \frac{\partial L}{\partial q} = \begin{pmatrix} m\ddot{x} \\ m\ddot{y} \\ I\ddot{\theta} \end{pmatrix} + \begin{pmatrix} 0 \\ mg \\ 0 \end{pmatrix}$$

Using equation 18 and factoring the mass/acceleration terms, equation 10 can now be written in the form:

19)

$$\begin{pmatrix} m & 0 & 0 \\ 0 & m & 0 \\ 0 & 0 & I \end{pmatrix}\begin{pmatrix} \ddot{x} \\ \ddot{y} \\ \ddot{\theta} \end{pmatrix} + \begin{pmatrix} 0 \\ mg \\ 0 \end{pmatrix} + \Phi_q^T \lambda = Q$$

The constraint terms in the above equation remain to be detailed, but it should be evident to the reader at this point that the other terms are "force" in nature, depending as they do on coordinate accelerations and gravity.

The pendulum constraints are expressed by the vector loop equation (ref. figure 8):

20)

$$\vec{R} - (\vec{A} - \vec{r}) = 0$$

This can be re-written in vector format as the (algebraic) constraint function:

21)

$$\vec{\Phi}(x, y, \theta) = (x + r_1 - A_1)\hat{i} + (y + r_2 + A_2)\hat{j} = 0$$

Where the *i* and *j* unit vectors are in ground.

In matrix notation, equation 20 becomes:

22)

$$\Phi(x, y, \theta) = \begin{pmatrix} x - A_1 - l\cos\theta \\ y - A_2 - l\sin\theta \end{pmatrix} = 0$$

Where l is the (constant) length of the vector $\vec{r}$. The Lagrange formulation (equation 10) employs the matrix formed by taking the partial derivatives of equation 22 with respect to the coordinates (i.e., the Jacobian), which yields the 2 by 3 array:

23)

$$\Phi_q = \begin{pmatrix} 1 & 0 & l\sin\theta \\ 0 & 1 & -l\cos\theta \end{pmatrix}$$

These constraints are now coupled to the system equations of motion by:

24)

$$\Phi_q^T \lambda = \begin{pmatrix} 1 & 0 \\ 0 & 1 \\ l\sin\theta & -l\cos\theta \end{pmatrix} \begin{pmatrix} \lambda_1 \\ \lambda_2 \end{pmatrix} = \begin{pmatrix} \lambda_1 \\ \lambda_2 \\ l\lambda_1\sin\theta - l\lambda_2\cos\theta \end{pmatrix}$$

Inserting these values into equation 19 and collecting like terms, one arrives at the initial value problem of 5 equations in 5 unknowns:

25)

$$\left. \begin{matrix} m\ddot{x} + \lambda_1 \\ m\ddot{y} + \lambda_2 \\ I\ddot{\theta} + \lambda_1 l\sin\theta - \lambda_2 l\cos\theta \\ x - A_1 - l\cos\theta \\ y - A_2 - l\sin\theta \end{matrix} \right\} = 0$$

Equation set 25 is a mixed set of differential and algebraic equations (DAEs) and the system model is, in theory, solvable in this form. However, one issue remains. The differential equations are 2nd order, while the solvers employed by Adams are 1st order. To leap this hurdle, additional velocity variables and the appropriate, defining equations are added to reduce the system to 1st order:

26)

$$u = \dot{x}$$
$$v = \dot{y}$$
$$\omega = \dot{\theta}$$

Inserting these expressions into equation set 25, one arrives at:

27)

$$\left.\begin{array}{c} m\dot{u} + \lambda_1 \\ m\dot{v} + \lambda_2 + mg \\ I\dot{\omega} + \lambda_1 l\sin\theta - \lambda_2 l\cos\theta \\ \dot{x} - u \\ \dot{y} - v \\ \dot{\theta} - \omega \\ x - A_1 - l\cos\theta \\ y - A_2 - l\sin\theta \end{array}\right\} = 0$$

Equation set 27 now represents the physics of the simple pendulum using a mixed set of differential and algebraic equations (DAEs) for the eight unknowns:

28)

$$\begin{pmatrix} u \\ v \\ \omega \\ x \\ y \\ \theta \\ \lambda_1 \\ \lambda_2 \end{pmatrix}$$

It should, perhaps, be mentioned that the spatial variables in equation set 28 correspond to the q's in equation 1, while the lambda's represent the Lagrange multipliers.

The differential equations are 1st order, and the system, as a whole, is nonlinear.

Solving the Equations

The DAEs in equation set 27 can be concisely expressed as:

29)

$$G(Y, \dot{Y}, t) = 0$$

where:

30)

$$Y = \begin{pmatrix} u \\ v \\ \omega \\ x \\ y \\ \theta \\ \lambda_1 \\ \lambda_2 \end{pmatrix}"$$

The expression for **Y** above is referred to as the "state" vector of the system. It should be pointed out that, in general usage, "state" vectors do not include such things as Lagrange multipliers, although that is being done here.

The transformation of the equations of set 29 into an explicit system of ordinary differential equations (ODEs), while difficult, can be done, but, besides bearing with it the potential disadvantage of resulting in an explicit, numerically "stiff" (as described earlier), ODE problem, it is not necessary. Adams will solve the equations in their implicit form.

The Adams solution consists of the determination of **Y** at discrete points in time:

31)

$$t_0 < t_1 < \cdots < t_{n-1} < t_n < \cdots < t_{END}$$

The distribution of the times given in equation 31 need not be uniform. A solution to equation set 27 at step j is given by:

32)

$$G\left(Y_j, \dot{Y}_j, t_j\right) = 0; j = 0,1,\cdots,n-1$$

If j is 0 (i.e., the starting solution time t=0.0), the solution prediction is based exclusively on the system initial conditions; otherwise the solver being used specifies a value for the time step based on the polynomial-based evaluation of previously-converged states, specifying a value for

33)

$$h = t_n - t_{n-1}$$

.....and computing a solution to

34)

$$G\left(Y_n, \dot{Y}_n, t_n\right) = 0$$

.....to within a given error tolerance

35)

$$\epsilon > 0.0$$

For each of the entries in Y, a predictor polynomial of order k is formed from initial conditions if just starting or by interpolation from previously converged values. The predictor polynomials estimate the value of each unknown and its first derivative at time t_n. The predicted values are generated independently for each component after which the Newton-Raphson algorithm is used to *simultaneously* correct the values. The reader is referred back to figure 2. However, now, instead of a single q and a 1 by 1 Jacobian J, our pendulum, as it currently stands, will have 8 q's and an 8 by 8 Jacobian. The corrected values are compared to the predicted values to see if they comply with the error tolerance specified in equation 35. The difference between the predicted and corrected values is also used to estimate the optimum time step and the optimum order for the predictor polynomials and

backward differencing formulas. If the error tolerance is satisfied, Adams proceeds to the next integration step with the improved values of the time step and order. If the error tolerance is not satisfied, the code backs up to the last converged step, and tries again with modified (usually reduced) values of time step h and polynomial order k.

The successive approximations to the solution of equation set 34 take the form

36)

$$G\left(Y_n^{(m)}, \frac{Y_n^{(m)} - Y_{n-1}}{h}, t_n\right) = 0$$

Where m denotes the corrector step for which

37)

$$Y_n^{(m)} = Y_n^{(m-1)} + \Delta$$

Iteration, denoted by m, continues until

38)

$$\|\Delta\| < s\epsilon$$

Where s is a scale factor dependent on the order of the predictor polynomials currently being used, ϵ is the error tolerance specified by the user, and $\|\Delta\|$ is the norm of the array of corrections.

The increment d at each iteration is given by the solution to the linearized system

39)

$$J\Delta = -G\left(y_n^{(m)}, \frac{y_n^{(m)} - y_{n-1}}{h}, t_n\right) = 0$$

The expression above is a more detailed form of equation 6 for which J is the Jacobian matrix for the column matrix of functions G. The Jacobian itself has the form

40)

$$\begin{pmatrix} m\dfrac{\partial \dot{u}}{\partial u} & & & & & & 1 & \\ & m\dfrac{\partial (\dot{v}+g)}{\partial v} & & & & & & 1 \\ & & I\dfrac{\partial \dot{\omega}}{\partial \omega} & & & & l\sin\theta & -l\cos\theta \\ -1 & & & \dfrac{\partial \dot{x}}{\partial x} & & & & \\ & -1 & & & \dfrac{\partial \dot{y}}{\partial y} & & & \\ & & -1 & & & \dfrac{\partial \dot{\theta}}{\partial \theta} & & \\ & & & 1 & & l\sin\theta & & \\ & & & & 1 & -l\cos\theta & & \end{pmatrix}$$

The entries not specified in the matrix above are identically zero. It should be noted that equation set 40 is "sparsely" populated. The 8 X 8 Jacobian has 64 entries of which only 17 are non-zero. Thus, the Jacobian is 26.5% sparse.

The backward differentiation formula (BDF)

41)

$$\dot{q} \approx \frac{q - q_{n-1}}{h}$$

defines the numerical relationship between a generalized coordinate and its first derivative. From equation 41, the expression for a first order BDF is

42)

$$\frac{\partial \dot{q}}{\partial q} = \frac{1}{h}$$

for each unknown in the state vector. Employing this definition, the Jacobian matrix becomes

43)

$$J = \begin{pmatrix} \dfrac{m}{h} & & & & & & & 1 & \\ & \dfrac{m}{h} & & & & & & & 1 \\ & & \dfrac{l}{h} & & & & & l\sin\theta & -l\cos\theta \\ -1 & & & \dfrac{1}{h} & & & & & \\ & -1 & & & \dfrac{1}{h} & & & & \\ & & -1 & & & \dfrac{1}{h} & & & \\ & & & 1 & & & \dfrac{1}{h} & & \\ & & & & 1 & & l\sin\theta & & \\ & & & & & 1 & -l\cos\theta & & \end{pmatrix}$$

for the first-order, backward differentiation formula. If higher-order approximating polynomials are in play, equation 42 becomes

44)

$$\frac{\partial \dot{q}}{\partial q} = \frac{1}{\beta h}$$

where the value of β depends on the order of the formula.

While the corrector convergence must satisfy the inequality given in equation 35, the time step and predictor order are determined by the integration error tolerance ϵ. Also, the integration error is filtered by the Adams implementation of the Gear integrator (called GSTIFF in Adams parlance), resulting in some of the state variables being omitted from the truncation error assessment.

At each integration step, the new time step h_{new} and the order k are determined by finding the maximum vales for h_{new} and the corresponding k that will satisfy

45)

$$C^{(k)} \left\| D\left(Y^{(p)} - Y^{(c)}\right) \right\| \left(\frac{h_{new}}{h_{previous}}\right)^{k+1} < \epsilon$$

The norm of the difference between the predicted values $Y^{(p)}$ and the corrected values $Y^{(c)}$, masked by the diagonal selection matrix D, is used to estimate the truncation error at the new time step. The constant $C^{(k)}$ is dependent on the order k and the mask for the integration error is

46)

$$D = \begin{pmatrix} 0 & & & & & & \\ & 0 & & & & & \\ & & 0 & & & & \\ & & & 1 & & & \\ & & & & 1 & & \\ & & & & & 1 & \\ & & & & & & 0 \\ & & & & & & & 0 \end{pmatrix}$$

for the pendulum state vector given in equation 29. Thus, for our pendulum, the integration error tolerance applies only to *x*, *y*, and *θ*. This has the consequence that, after the integration is "converged," velocities are back-calculated using

47)

$$\dot{q} = \frac{\Delta q}{h}$$

and accelerations are back-calculated as

48)

$$\ddot{q} = \frac{\Delta q}{h^2}$$

The motion of the simple, 2D pendulum described above is driven exclusively by the acceleration field due to gravity. The three differential equations in equation set 19 govern the motion in a manner which must comply with the two independent constraint equations in equation set 22.

The Gruebler Expression for a 2D Model

When developing an MBD model in Adams, it is always important to anticipate the system's degree of freedom (DOF) count and, equally important, to understand it. An important tool in determining this is the Gruebler Equation. For a model in two-dimensional (2D) space, this takes the form

49)

$$DOF = 3 * (N_{PARTS} - 1) - N_{CONSTRAINTS}$$

Where N_{PARTS} is the total number of independent bodies (Adams PARTs) in the model, inclusive of the ground part, and $N_{CONSTRAINTS}$ is the number of algebraic constraints present in the system. For our model, with 2 parts (the arm and ground) and 2 constraints, λ_1 and λ_2. This computes to 1, as expected. A word of caution is needed. Fulfillment of the Gruebler expression represents a necessary, but not sufficient, indicator of a model's true DOF count. It is possible to have, say, a redundant constraint at one location in a model and a missing constraint at another location. The Gruebler count would be correct, but the solution would likely fail or, at least, yield incorrect results.

Addition of a Restraint

The dynamic motion permitted by an Adams model is, in a sense, shared by the generalized coordinates. Thus, the single degree of freedom of our pendulum belongs jointly to the three displacement variables x, y, and θ.

If additional, external forces are added to the system, the behavior of the system will, in general, be subject to change.

In the figure below, we assume that a torsional spring-damper, depicted as a clock spring, is added to the pendulum hinge.

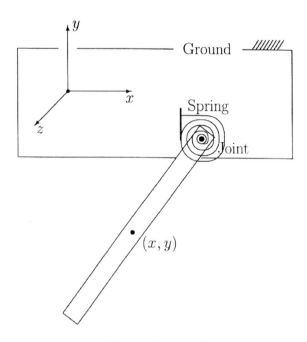

Figure 9 2D Pendulum with Added Torsional Restraint

A torsional force, will, in general, effect the angular acceleration of the parts to which it is applied. In general form, the vector equation for such a spring is given by

50)

$$\vec{T}_f + \left[K_T(\theta - \theta_0) + C_T\dot{\theta}\right]\hat{k} = 0$$

Where K_T is the torsional spring constant; C_T is the torsional damping coefficient, θ_0 is the no-load angle of the torsional spring, and $\hat{k}$ is the unit vector normal to the plane in which the torque is applied. Examination of equation set 27 reveals that it would be possible to directly modify the equation for $\dot{\omega}$. However, in addition to being difficult to program, this would impact the coefficient terms which have already been defined and make it difficult to separate out the torque value at any point in the solution. Rather than do this, a new equation and its variable are added, as shown below.

51)

$$\left.\begin{array}{c} m\dot{u} + \lambda_1 \\ m\dot{v} + \lambda_2 + mg \\ I\dot{\omega} + \lambda_1 l\sin\theta - \lambda_2 l\cos\theta - T_f \\ T_f + K_T(\theta - \theta_0) + C_T\omega \\ \dot{x} - u \\ \dot{y} - v \\ \dot{\theta} - \omega \\ x - A_1 - l\cos\theta \\ y - A_2 - l\sin\theta \end{array}\right\} = 0$$

The Jacobian for this system becomes

52)

$$\begin{pmatrix} m\dfrac{\partial\dot{u}}{\partial u} & & & & & 1 & & & \\ & m\dfrac{\partial(\dot{v}+g)}{\partial v} & & & & & 1 & & \\ & & I\dfrac{\partial\dot{\omega}}{\partial\omega} & & & l\sin\theta & -l\cos\theta & -1 \\ & & & C_T & & K_T & & 1 \\ -1 & & & & \dfrac{\partial\dot{x}}{\partial x} & & & \\ & -1 & & & & \dfrac{\partial\dot{y}}{\partial y} & & \\ & & -1 & & & & \dfrac{\partial\dot{\theta}}{\partial\theta} & \\ & & & 1 & & & l\sin\theta & \\ & & & 1 & & & -l\cos\theta & \end{pmatrix}$$

Lest the reader become concerned about the "profligate" addition of equations and variables, it must be remembered that Adams is designed to exploit equation set sparseness. The addition of the torque has added four terms to the Jacobian for a total of 21. But the Jacobian is now a 9 X 9 array, yielding a sparseness of 25.9%. This is a rather modest improvement in sparseness, but, as we shall see when we move our pendulum to the Adams 3 dimensional space, the gains become more significant.

Addition of a Constraint (or reduction to ZERO DOFs)

The motion of the free-swinging pendulum (i.e., the 1st model without the hinge restraint) is approximately sinusoidal only for very low-amplitude oscillatory motion. We can, however, compel this motion to be perfectly sinusoidal by imposing further restrictions on the pendulum arm. The figure below shows our pendulum to which a sinusoidally oscillating, slotted guide has been added which traps the pendulum mass center in its slot, thereby constraining its motion in the X-direction.

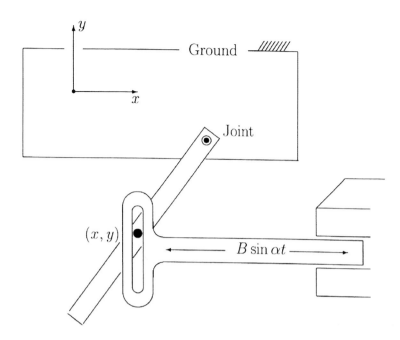

Figure 10 2D Pendulum with CG Constrained in the Ground X-direction

Although the additional modeling components could be added to model the slotted guide part and its additional constraints, this is not necessary. Instead, a generalized constraint between ground and the arm CG will be employed which compels the pendulum arm to move as we require. The slot constraint can be expressed as

53)

$$\lambda_3 - (x - A_1 - B\sin\alpha t) = 0$$

Adding this constraint definition to the system equations results in

54)

$$\left.\begin{array}{c} m\dot{u} + \lambda_1 \\ m\dot{v} + \lambda_2 + mg \\ I\dot{\omega} + \lambda_1 l\sin\theta - \lambda_2 l\cos\theta - T_f \\ T_f + K_T(\theta - \theta_0) + C_T\omega \\ \dot{x} - u \\ \dot{y} - v \\ \dot{\theta} - \omega \\ x - A_1 - l\cos\theta \\ y - A_2 - l\sin\theta \\ x - A_1 - B\sin\alpha t \end{array}\right\} = 0$$

This addition results in a fundamental change in the nature of the problem. The Gruebler DOF count is zero, indicating that the number of independent constraint conditions now equals the number of generalized coordinates. It is no longer a dynamics problem and has become a kinematics problem for which the integration with time of the differential variables is no longer needed. Leaving them in the

solution set will cause them to be computed, but their values have no influence on the arm displacement histories.

Beginning with an initial estimate of the values of

55)

$$\begin{pmatrix} x \\ y \\ \theta \end{pmatrix}$$

A Newton-Raphson algorithm will be used to solve for the mechanism position at any given time. The Jacobian matrix for just the constraint equations in equation set 54 is

56)

$$\begin{pmatrix} 1 & 0 & l\sin\theta \\ 0 & 1 & -l\cos\theta \\ 1 & 0 & 0 \end{pmatrix}$$

The kinematic solution generates values for just the displacement variables in expression 55.

To compute values for the remaining elements of the state vector Y, the constraint equations are differentiated (i.e., numerically differenced) once and evaluated using the displacement variables to obtain the velocities. Next, the equations are differenced a second time to obtain the accelerations. Finally, the force balance equations are utilized to determine the values of the constraint forces.

Next, we will run the problems detailed above in Adams.

The 3D Pendulum in Adams

In the theory above, the pendulum has been analyzed in a two dimensional space permitting X translation, Y translation, and theta Z rotations. Adams, however, assumes a three-dimensional space for all modeling. Thus, the equation set detailed above will have to be expanded to include Z translation and the two remaining rotations. In addition, the equation set will be further modified for the sake of numerical expediency.

Adams Features Introduced in this Model:

1) **Part**
2) **Revolute Joint**
3) **Single Component Force (SFORCE, in this case rotational)**
4) **The generalized constraint (GCON)**
5) **Transient dynamic and kinematic solution modes**

Free Pendulum

The figure below shows a simple pendulum, constrained to move in the XY plane, rendered in MKS units.

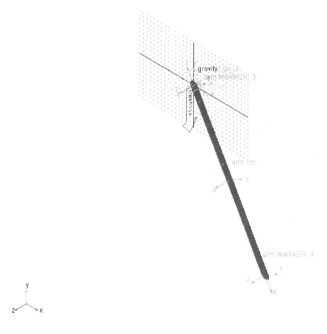

Figure 11 Adams 3D Pendulum

The pendulum arm has the following properties:

1) It is constrained to ground at the origin by a 5-constraint revolute joint (i.e., a hinge)
2) It is a steel, prismatic bar with rounded ends. It is built as an Adams solid link component dimensioned 2 meters long (between rounded end centers), 0.1 meters wide, and 0.005 meters thick
3) It is displaced +30 degrees about global Z from the vertical and gravity acts in the global negative Y-direction

The resulting mass properties are shown below:

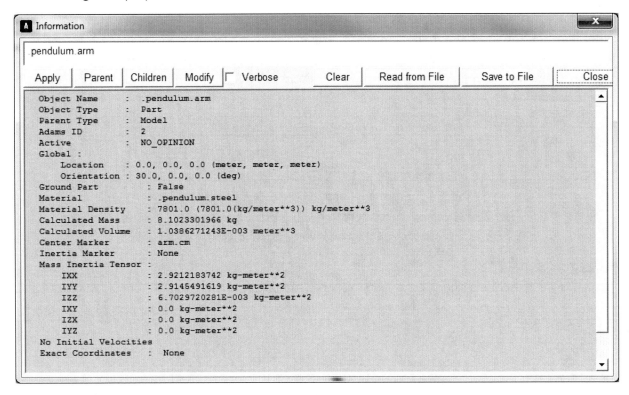

Figure 12 Adams 3D Pendulum Arm Mass Properties

The table below identifies the equations and variables, as reported by the Adams solver, defining the behavior of the dynamic degree of freedom (Psi) of the 3D pendulum body. It should be noted that an Adams user rarely, if ever, has to examine the model this deeply. Indeed, for most practical models, the equation set map can quickly become somewhat overwhelming, rendering it of little use. However, for this very simple 3D pendulum example it is useful to show the model structure so that it can be contrasted with the simplified 2D example detailed previously.

Equation Number	Function	Variable Number	Variable	Comment
1	X Force	1	X Velocity	
2	Y Force	2	Y Velocity	
3	Z Force	3	Z Velocity	
4	Psi Momentum	4	Psi Velocity	
5	Phi Momentum	5	Phi Velocity	
6	Theta Momentum	6	Theta Velocity	
7	Psi Torque	7	Psi Momentum	
8	Phi Torque	8	Phi Momentum	
9	Theta Torque	9	Theta Momentum	
10	X Velocity	10	X	
11	Y Velocity	11	Y	
12	Z Velocity	12	Z	
13	Psi Velocity	13	Psi	Independent variable

14	Phi Velocity	14	Phi	
15	Theta Velocity	15	Theta	
16	X Displacement	16	X Lambda	
17	Y Displacement	17	Y Lambda	
18	Z Displacement	18	Z Lambda	
19	Zi dot Xj	19	Lambda Dot 1	Vector Scalar
20	Zi dot Yj	20	Lambda Dot 2	Vector Scalar

Table 2 Equation/Variable Map of 3D Pendulum Body

Examination of the data above reveals that there are now 20 equations and variables instead of the 8 generated for the 2D model. The changes and additions are listed below:

1) The rotation of the pendulum body about in the XY plane is given by the Euler angle Psi instead of rotation angle Theta from the 2D model (note: more detail on the Body-based 313 rotation angles …Psi, Theta, Phi…employed by Adams is given below).
2) A single Z-force equation dependent on the Z-direction translational displacement has been added.
3) A single Z-velocity equation has been added.
4) Two angular velocity equations have been added.
5) Two angular torques have been added.
6) Three angular momentum equations have been added.
7) Three constraint Lambda equations have been added to fix the pendulum pin in the Z-direction, together with 2 off-axis (rotational) lambdas defined by requiring the vector dot products of the reference J marker X- and Y-axes with the displacing I marker Z-axis to be zero (i.e., orthogonal).

All in all, 12 additional equations are needed to "convert" the 2D model to 3D, bringing the total to 20. The need for the additional displacement and velocity variables in the added dimensions should be obvious, but why, one might ask, introduce additional angular momentum equations? The answer to this lies in the nature of the inertia terms. For the 2D model, the arm can move in the XY plane only, and the value of the inertia I is unchanging with theta. For a **general** 3D PART, the potential exists for all three rotational coordinates to vary. While this can't happen for our constrained pendulum arm because of the nature of its hinge constraints, Adams must be predicated so that it can, if necessary, gyrate wildly about all three axes. In which event, the instantaneous, **globally-referenced**, and generally highly nonlinear values of I, would have to be continuously re-computed at each solution step. This would be very costly computationally, so numerical efficiencies are sought wherever possible. The body torques are much better behaved when expressed in terms of momenta.

Note: this model and the variations that follow will all be run for 10 simulation seconds at an output rate of 1000 output steps per second using the GSTIFF SI2 integrator with ERROR set to 1.0E-5.

The figure below gives the time history of the pendulum angular velocity.

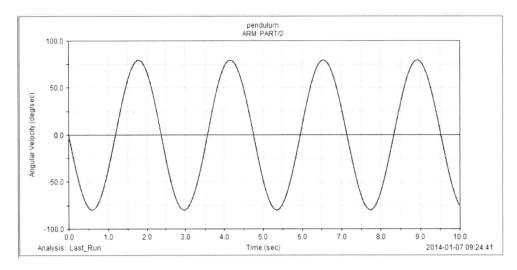

Figure 13 Free-Hanging Adams 3D Pendulum Angular Velocity History -- DOF Count = 1

It should be noted that, for this model, the Adams solver reports 81 entries in the 20 X 20 Jacobian array, yielding a sparsity of 20.2%. Thus, adding the additional dimension to our pendulum problem has improved this important factor.

Restraint Added

In our 2D exposition, a restraint in the form of a torsional spring-damper was added to the pendulum hinge. This will be done for the 3D pendulum by applying a torque to the hinge of the form:

57)

$$T = -KT * \theta - CT * \omega$$

In the expression above, KT is the torsional stiffness of the spring and CT is the corresponding torsional damping. In the model, KT has been set to 1.0 Newton-meter/radian and CT to 1.0 Newton-meter-seconds/radian. The modified pendulum schematic is shown below.

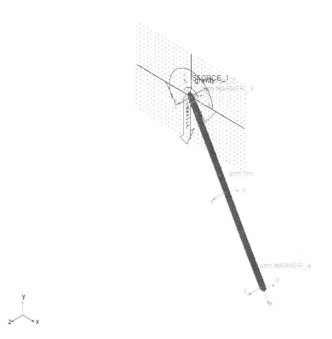

Figure 14 Adams 3D Pendulum with Torsional Restraint Added to Hinge

The only change to the equation set is the addition of the torque equation and variable shown in table 3 below.

Equation Number	Function	Variable Number	Variable	Comment
21	Torque	21	Torque	Cross-coupling terms added to previous equations 4,7, and 13

Table 3 Additional Equation and Variable Due to Added Hinge Torque

The pendulum velocity and restraint histories are given below.

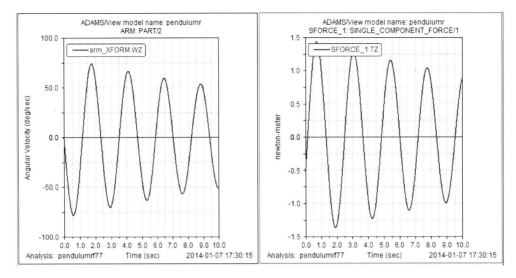

Figure 15 Restrained Adams 3D Pendulum Velocity and Restraint Torque Histories – DOF Count =1

For this model, the solver declares 21 equations with 91 entries for a sparsity of 20.6%.

Constraint Added

Next, an algebraic, generalized constraint (GCON) will be employed to apply a sinusoidally-varying displacement motion in the X-direction on the pendulum arm mass center. This GCON has the basic form of the constraint added to the 2D pendulum but will start the pendulum from the +30 degree, displaced position and will be scaled to mimic the free-swinging 3D pendulum above. To accomplish this, the GCON takes the form:

58)

$$\lambda = DX(I, J, R) + Do * sin\big(\omega * (t + \phi)\big) = 0.0$$

Where:

1) *DX(I,J,R)* is the variable *x*-displacement of the I-MARKER (the arm center of mass - CM) with respect to the J-MARKER (hinge) measures in the *R* coordinate system (0 → ground)
2) *Do* is the initial CM offset (+0.5 m)
3) *w* is the displacement frequency (+2.65 Hz)
4) *t* is the simulation time (seconds)
5) *Phi* is the phase angle shift factor(6.526)

Equation Number	Function	Variable Number	Variable	Comment
22	X Force	22	GCON Lambda	Cross-coupling terms added to previous equations 1, 10, and 13

Table 4: Additional Equation and Variable Due to Added Generalized Constraint

The figures below summarize the behavior of the Adams 3D pendulum with a torsion spring restraint on the hinges and an oscillating, translational constraint on the pendulum arm mass center.

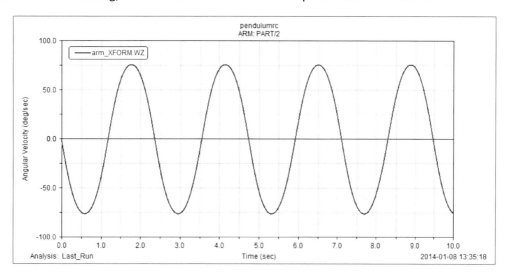

Figure 16: 3D Pendulum (Restrained and Constrained) Rotational Velocity History—DOF Count = 0

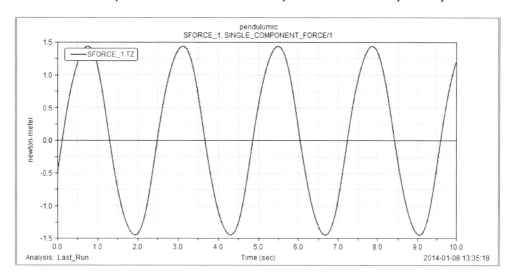

Figure 17: 3D Pendulum (Restrained and Constrained) Restraint History – DOF Count = 0

41

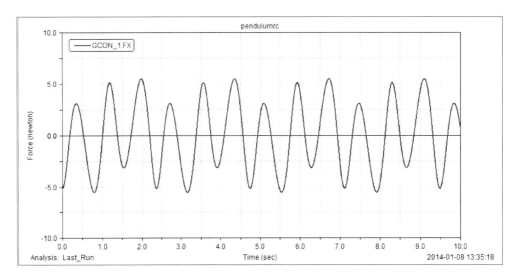

Figure 18: 3D Pendulum (Restrained and Constrained) GCON Constraint History – DOF Count = 0

A comparison of the angular displacement histories of all three versions of the Adams pendulum models is in order.

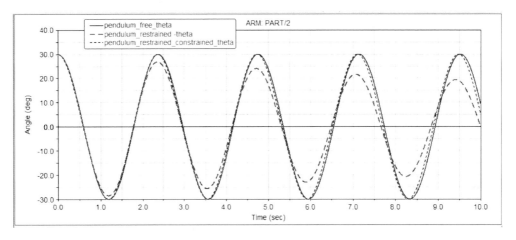

Figure 19 Comparison -- Pendulum Angular Displacements -- All 3 Runs

The figure below compares the true, nonlinear, integrated motion of the pendulum arm with the forced, constraint-based motion.

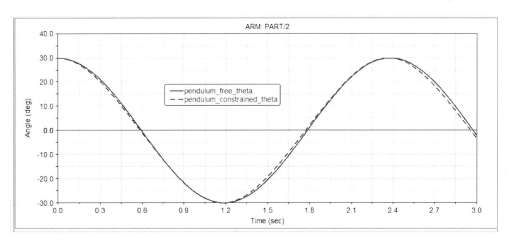

Figure 20 Pendulum Cycle Comparison -- True Non-Linear vs Constrained Non-Linear

Comments Concerning the Adams 3D Pendulum Models

1) Although somewhat diminutive, the use of a simple pendulum provides a potential Adams user a model which is nevertheless highly informative and, hopefully, supplies a sense of the computational sophistication upon which Adams is based.

2) As anticipated, the addition of a modest spring-damper causes the pendulum motion to decay linearly with time.

3) The generalized constraint (GCON) imposes motion that results in model behavior which closely mimics the free-hanging system. However, closer scrutiny of the comparison plot (figure 20) reveals that the true pendulum motion is, in a somewhat subtle fashion, more complex and does not result in a true sinusoid.

4) The addition of a time-dependent, horizontal constraint using a GCON forces the motion back to full amplitude, regardless of the restraint on the hinge. It must be emphasized that, to satisfy a constraint, a Lagrange multiplier will provide whatever force is necessary, no matter how large it may become.

5) Initially, all models were executed using the "dynamic" keyword in the simulation command. The Adams software is intelligent enough to warn the user that, for the final model, the use of the "kinematic" keyword in lieu of "dynamic" would result in a more efficient solution. Requesting a dynamic solution for a zero DOF problem causes the code to solve in time using the complete equation set, even though the differential terms are no longer independent and do not affect the solution. As emphasized in the 2D theory example above, a kinematic model uses the constraint equation subset *only* to solve through time. Generating the values of any forces in the model becomes numerically trivial. Switching to 'kinematic' results in a 47% reduction in solution time.

Concerning the Euler Angles

A plethora of potential schemes exist for tracking angular motion in 3D space. Unfortunately, all of them are complicated and can be confusing. Long ago, when gyroscope theory was in its infancy, Euler angles were the representation of choice, employing as they do the minimum number of variables (three for a second order solver, six if the solution order is reduced to 1). Further, these angular representations permit reference axes to be either fixed in the inertial reference frame or to be fixed to the body and allow the formulations to be sequenced about the chosen axes as desired. Adams employs body-fixed 313 Euler rotations. The body right-handed (dextral) triad is subjected to rotations taking place *sequentially* about the body z, x', and z'' axes (see figure below).

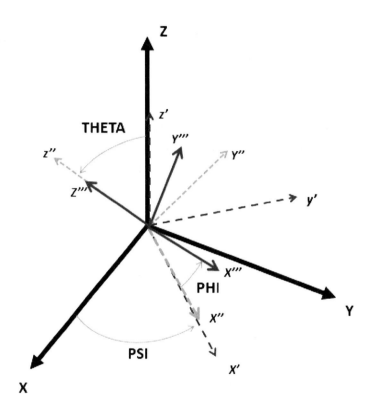

Figure 21 Euler Body 313 Angle Sequence

Each of the triads in the figure is right-handed and orthogonal. The body triad is initially co-aligned with the reference triad (black), and, for convenience, starts off coincident with it as well, although coincidence (or the lack thereof) plays no role in the angular transformations and has been used here only to simplify the figure. After the **PSI** rotation about the un-primed Z-axis, the first body position is shown by the red triad (with single primes). The next rotation is **THETA** about the *x'* axis, after which the body has assumed the position of the green triad (with double primes on the axes). The final rotation is **PHI** about the *z''* axis, resulting in the blue triad (with triple primes on the axes). This is the final position.

It should be clear from the figure that, in general, the angles associated with the Euler triple are not orthogonal. In other words, the summation of the rotational pseudo-vectors along the z, x' and z'' directions generally has no meaning. There is, however, a more important consideration to keep in

mind. Any time **THETA** goes to zero in a body 313 transformation, the expression for the **PSI** velocity becomes singular due to the existence of a **sin(THETA)** term in the denominator [3, page 63]. This is classically referred to as the "gimbal lock" condition. The gimbal lock singularity issue can be avoided by the use of alternative rotational tracking such as is available using somewhat abstract mathematical entities known as "quaternions." However, while generally well-defined, quaternions bring an appreciable increase in the computational overhead and can be subject to severe scaling problems. This has led the developers of Adams to persist with the use of Euler angles with coding added to avoid singularity problems. As any **THETA** approaches within a certain margin of zero, the rotating coordinate system is re-oriented using an Euler transformation for **PSI, THETA** and **PHI** of (90, 90, 0) degrees and any effected quantities are appropriately shuffled to avoid changing the physical definition of the problem. The original orientation is then restored after the danger has passed. However, this requires a system "re-factorization," which is, generally, computationally costly. If a model is constantly re-factorizing, it may be ill-posed. Say, for example, that the center of mass (CM) marker in a car model tire were oriented such that its Z-axis lay in the plane of the wheel and global Z was perpendicular to the road surface. As the vehicle moved along, the tire CM Z-axis would repeatedly threaten alignment with global Z, potentially requiring repeated re-factorization. Fixed (initial) alignments are not a problem, however. In the Adams pendulum model, initial Z-alignment is present in both the hinge and CM markers. The Adams coding addresses this issue at the start and doesn't need to re-factorize.

Some Example Problems

A Statement:

> *"If it moves, and you want to know how much, and what the forces are, you should use Adams"* —Anonymous

The bold statement above is not mere hyperbole. Adams has been employed to gain insight into the behavior of systems running the gamut from 1-piece, orbiting satellites to bullet trains speeding onto flexible overpass trestles. Due to limits on the size of this book, it is not practical to detail Adams models of any substantial size. Nonetheless, it is hoped that the three rather modest examples which follow will provide the reader with some ideas of the substantial capabilities of the Adams MBD software. The samples selected include:

1) A fourbar linkage (and what can go wrong with it).
2) A backhoe excavator (with an FEA-generated, flexible boom) performing a cut/swing/dump duty cycle.
3) An automotive differential being loaded in a turn (generated by the Adams/Machinery vertical application).

All of the variations of the first example are rather small but introduce some important effects related to constraint modeling. The excavator model starts off rather simply but evolves into moderate complexity with the introduction of a component rendered flexible using an FEA-derived flexible part. It creeps into somewhat deeper complexity with a simplified example of the pseudo modeling of mass variability. The differential model delves into the world of vertical applications by employing the User-Defined Element (UDE), which offers great utility at the cost of some loss in generality. The reader is strongly urged to take these problems *in sequence* and is further counseled to load the model versions delivered with this

book and use the Adams/View model browser freely to explore the models. Nor should the user be afraid to experiment with these models, since one often can learn more from doing something wrong than from exercising a model from which all the modeling mistakes have been expunged.

Most of the figures throughout this Examples section are screenshots from the Adams/View software package, which is the most common pre- and post-processor used for building models of mechanical systems with Adams.

Example 1 – Fourbar Linkage

Adams Features and Concepts in this Model:

1) **Parts**
2) **Joints (Revolute, Spherical, Universal)**
3) **Motion Constraint**
4) **Consistent Redundant Constraints**
5) **Inconsistent Redundant Constraints**
6) **Transient Singularities**

While relatively simple as a mechanism, the classical fourbar linkage is nonetheless a very important and often-used mechanical system. It serves also as an excellent learning tool. The figure below shows a fourbar system rendered in millimeter/kilogram/seconds (**mmks**) units (which are the default units for Adams/View).

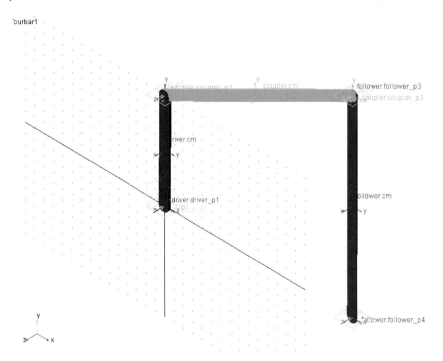

Figure 22 Fourbar Mechanism (Isometric View)

In brief:

1) The global origin of the system is located at the grid center.
2) For identification purposes, the connection points (i.e., JOINTs) are labeled p1 through p4 clockwise starting from the driver attachment to ground.
3) As input, the system lies in the global XY plane.
4) All CG locations and mass/inertia properties are generated by Adams/View from the link geometries using steel as the material specification.
5) The driver link (red) is 0.5 meters long, 50 mm wide, and 15 mm thick.
6) The follower link (blue) is 1 meter long, 50 mm wide, and 5 mm thick.
7) The coupler link (green) is 1.118 meters long, 50 mm wide, and 10 mm thick.
8) All hinges are (initially) specified as revolute joints.
9) The motion statement on the driver specifies a displacement of one revolution per second in the counterclockwise direction, and 360 output steps are requested.

Version 1 – Redundant but Consistent Constraints

When the fourbar was generated, the assumption was made that all the link connections could be represented as revolute joints similar in action to common door hinges. The hinge shown below connecting the coupler to the follower is typical.

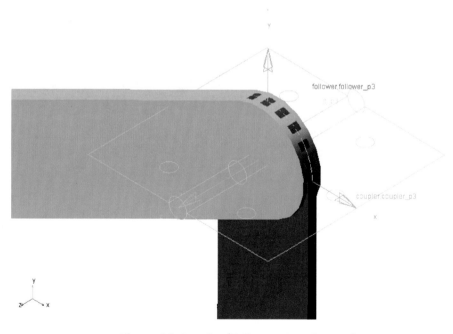

Figure 23 Coupler/Follower Revolute Joint

The model is executed using the simulation control shown below.

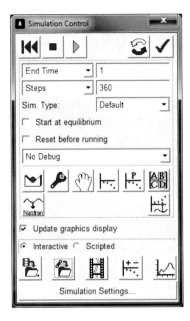

Figure 24 Fourbar Simulation Control

Thus, the driver will make 1 turn and results will be saved at 1 degree intervals.

The figure below uses "trace" commands to show the paths taken by the pin centers of the coupler.

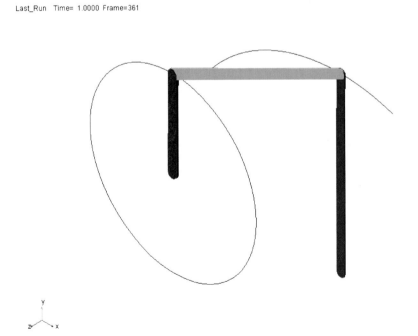

Figure 25 Coupler Pin Center Path Traces

The figure below gives the angular velocities of the driver and follower. The term XFORM in the plot legend refers to the LPRF of the part.

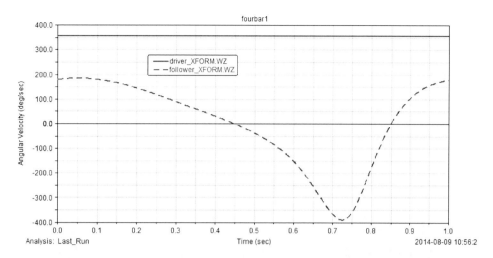

Figure 26 Driver and Follower Angular Velocities about Global Z

The Gruebler Expression for a 3D Model

The importance of the Gruebler expression was previously cited in the theory section for a theoretical 2D pendulum model. This concept will now be re-visited for the three dimensional (3D) fourbar linkage.

For a model in three-dimensional space, the Gruebler expression takes the form:

59)

$$DOF = 6 * (N_{PARTS} - 1) - N_{CONSTRAINTS}$$

Where N_{PARTS} is the total number of independent bodies (Adams PARTs) in the model, inclusive of the GROUND part, and $N_{CONSTRAINTS}$ is the number of algebraic constraints present in the system. For the fourbar system: Nparts = 4; Nconstraints = 21 (5 constraints per REVOLUTE joint plus 1 MOTION constraint). The Gruebler count computes to (+18 -21) = -3, signifying that there are 3 *redundant* constraints in the model! A "redundant" constraint duplicates one previously encountered in the system equation set. To confirm this, the Tools/Model/Verify command can be used to interrogate the system.

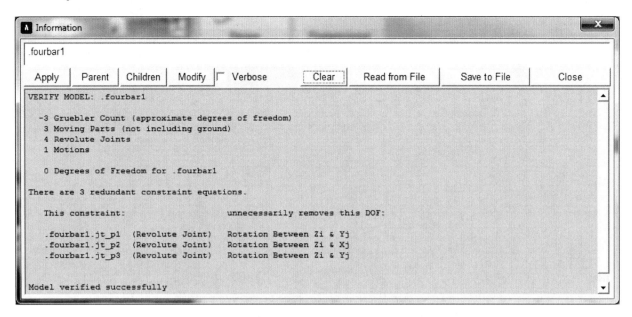

Figure 27 Fourbar Model Statistics Using Model Verify

Model statistics correctly identifies the redundancies, yet it runs the model successfully in spite of this. How can this be? The answer is as follows: If the excess constraints are *consistent* with one another, their numerical constraint functions in the problem constraint equations are mathematically identical and can be detected by Adams during the initial conditions analysis phase. In short, at the solution start, Adams eliminates any consistent redundancies and presses on. Will Adams always be able to thus rescue a solution? The answer is…not always.

Version 2 – Motion into a Non-Solvable State

Let us modify the fourbar by driving the system at the joint connecting the follower to ground. To accomplish this, the motion applied to the driver is simply deactivated and the same displacement function is applied to the follower. The figure below shows the motion constraint status using the model browser.

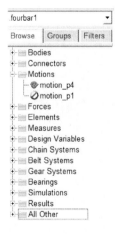

Figure 28 Status of Motion Constraints

The red circle with the diagonal bar shows that the driver motion at point p1 is not active.

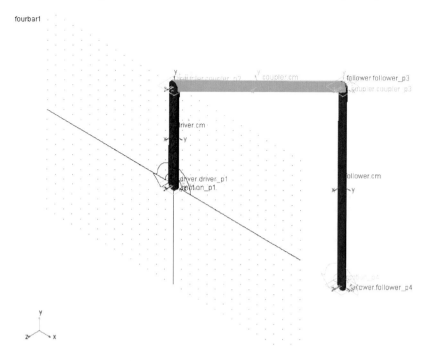

Figure 29 Fourbar: Driver Motion Deactivated, Follower Motion Added

After this change, the model solution starts, then fails! The failure messages returned by Adams are shown below.

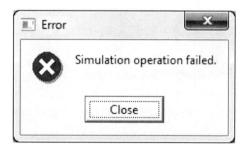

Figure 30 Failed Solution Warning

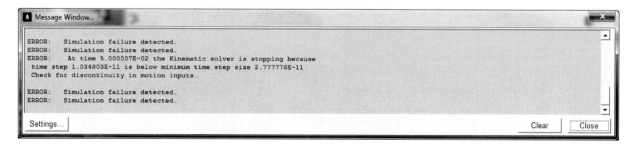

Figure 31 Failed Solution Message

The figure below clearly indicates what has happened.

.ast_Run   Time= 0.0500 Frame=19

Figure 32 Motion into Constraint Failure

Because the follower is twice as long as the driver, the system quickly moves into a position where the driver and coupler have "straight-lined." Consequently, the follower cannot continue to satisfy the rotational motion constraint driving it without violating other constraints in the system. The system constraints have become incompatible.

A Joint Subtlety

An alert reader may have noticed something else. Although the same motion function was applied to drive the follower as was originally applied to the driver, it moves in the opposite direction! What is going on here? The answer is somewhat subtle and depends on the joint specification used. In an Adams joint, motion always has the sense of "move the I MARKER relative to the J MARKER." Using the Adams/View "Info" utility, the two grounded joint specifications are shown below.

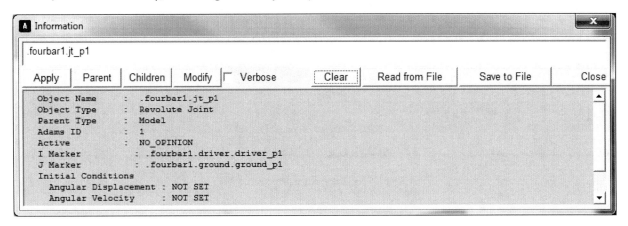

Figure 33 Driver/Ground Joint

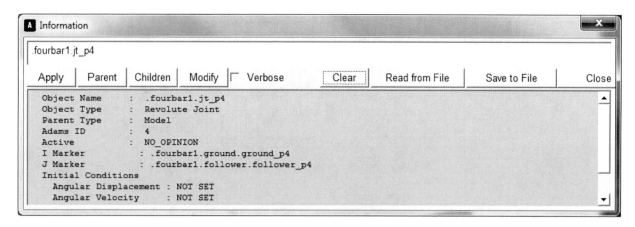

Figure 34 Ground/Follower Joint

Comparison shows that the driver/ground joint specifies the ground_p1 marker as the joint **J MARKER**, while the ground/follower joint specifies the ground_p4 marker as the **I MARKER**. Since ground is the model inertial reference frame, any marker fixed in ground cannot move. Thus, for the follower/ground joint, I stays put and J moves in the opposite direction. The motion direction can be made to move counterclockwise again by either changing the sign of the motion function or switching the I & J MARKER specifications in the joint definition.

Version 3 – Motion-Dependent Changes in DOF Count

The constraint sets of articulating mechanisms are quite capable of high chicanery. Let us next "square" the fourbar by increasing the length of the driver from 0.5 meters to 1.0 meters. Further, the follower motion will be deleted and the driver motion re-activated. The system is shown below.

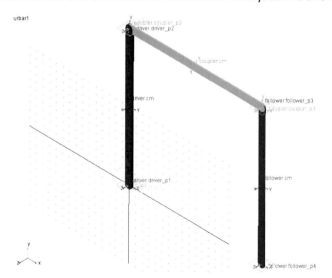

Figure 35 "Squared" Fourbar

It should be noted that, when using Adams/Views for these simple alterations to the model, the CG locations and mass properties of the driver and coupler are automatically updated correctly.

Upon execution, the solution fails when the lengthened driver attempts to reach 270 degrees. Why?

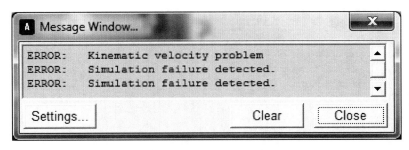

Figure 36 "Squared" Fourbar Solution Failure Message

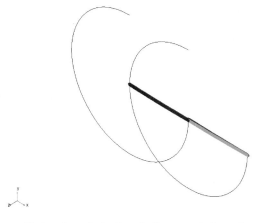

Figure 37 "Squared" Fourbar Solution Failure as Driver Approaches 270 Degrees

The reason is that, at precisely 270 degrees of driver rotation, the driver/coupler, coupler/follower, and follower/ground joints all become "focused," that is, coincident and co-aligned. At this precise position, there is nothing to prevent the coupler and follower from rotating about global Z *independently* of the driver. Entries on the main diagonal of the constraint set used to solve the system equations in time have gone numerically and irretrievably to zero. Referring back to the theory section, the system Jacobian has become singular and can no longer be inverted.

It should be noted that the system remains solvable when the driver reaches 90 degrees, even though three joints again become "focused," because one of the joints includes the driver motion which prevents the coupler and follower from losing their constraints about global Z.

_ast_Run   Time= 0.2500 Frame=091

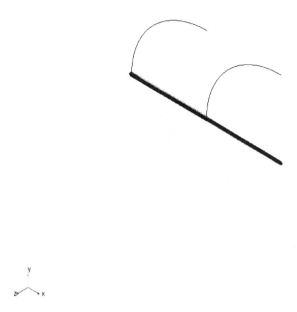

Figure 38 "Square" Fourbar with Driver at Precisely 90 Degrees

It is sometimes possible to use skullduggery to get a solution when one really shouldn't. If the number of solution steps requested is changed from 360 to, say, 361, the squared fourbar happily computes to completion! This "trivial" output step change prevents the equations from being numerically evaluated at precisely 270 degrees, and Adams never knows that it has passed (perhaps "jumped" is a better term) over a singular position*. **While one should be aware that seemingly unrelated parameter changes can lure a poorly-defined model to complete a solution, such trickery is strongly discouraged, since there is great peril in compelling flawed models to provide a solution regardless of their integrity! Just because it runs doesn't guarantee that it is correct!***

At this point, we will return to using the original fourbar with the 0.5 meter driver.

Version 4 – Redundant and Inconsistent Constraints

The initial fourbar model yielded a good solution, even though its constraint set contained 3 redundancies. The figure below shows the same fourbar, but with its driver attachment joint rotated 15 degrees off-axis with respect to the other 3 revolute joints.

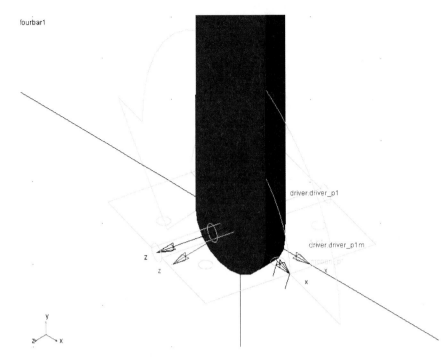

fourbar1

driver.driver_p1

driver.driver_p1m

Figure 39 Fourbar Model with Off-Angle Driver Joint

An attempt to execute this model immediately fails, yielding the message shown below.

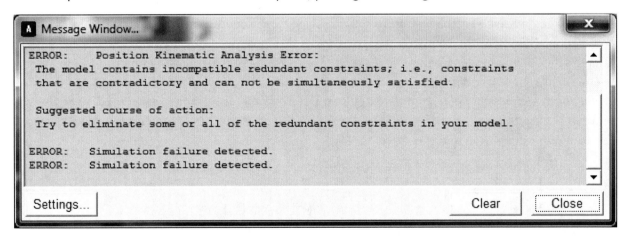

```
ERROR:    Position Kinematic Analysis Error:
The model contains incompatible redundant constraints; i.e., constraints
that are contradictory and can not be simultaneously satisfied.

Suggested course of action:
Try to eliminate some or all of the redundant constraints in your model.

ERROR:    Simulation failure detected.
ERROR:    Simulation failure detected.
```

Figure 40 Fourbar with Off-Angle Driver Joint: Failure Message

Adams has, again, clearly recognized the redundancy issue, but the code has no way of identifying which redundancies to eliminate. How is this issue resolved? The answer is basic: Even though Adams may tolerate constraint redundancies under special conditions, the user should *never* deliberately employ them. Redundant constraints are often a sign that the user doesn't really understand the mechanism being analyzed. Thus, it is axiomatic that *one should <u>always</u> try to eliminate any redundancies in a model constraint set*.

Clearly, there are many possible modifications to our model which would drive the system Gruebler count to zero. However, it must be remembered that a Gruebler count of zero is a *necessary* but not *sufficient* condition for a computable, 0 DOF model. The user may remove too many constraints at one

location and too few at another, so that the Gruebler count is numerically correct, but the constraint distribution is wrong.

The figures below shows the fourbar with the driver/coupler revolute switched to a spherical joint, and the coupler/follower revolute deactivated and replaced by a universal joint.

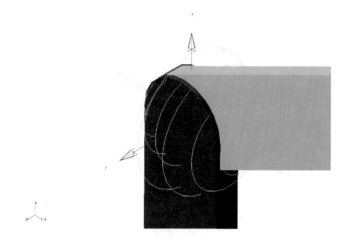

Figure 41 Driver/Coupler Spherical Joint

 It should be noted that the two Z-axes defining the universal joint must be orthogonal and represent the Cardan cross of a U-joint. This requires the addition of another marker (the red triad in the figure below) at the joint center. Further, because it is often mistakenly done, it should be emphasized that the Cardan cross plane must never lie in (or move into) the plane defined by axes of the coupler and the follower.

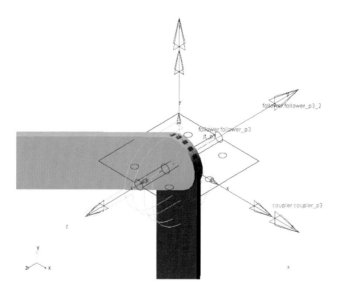

Figure 42 Coupler/Follower Connection -- Revolute Joint De-Activated, Universal Joint Added

Note: The logic behind the selection of the spherical and universal joints is as follows:

1) The spherical joint (providing 3 translational DOF constraints) keeps the driver and coupler from separating but does not eliminate any rotational DOFs. The Gruebler count at this point would be -1.

2) If another spherical joint were used at the coupler/follower connection, 2 more constraints would be eliminated, but the Gruebler count would be +1, and the coupler could spin about the axis defined by its 2 pin ends. The universal joint (providing 3 translational DOF constraints and 1 rotational DOF constraint) both pins the parts together and constrains the spin. The Gruebler count is now 0.

To enable numerical tracking of the coupler cm, a reference marker ("ground_origin_ref") is added to ground at the origin and a displacement request referring to it is generated.

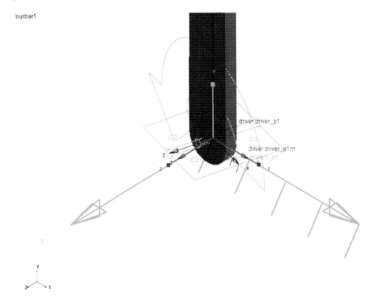

Figure 43 Reference marker (Green) at Ground Origin

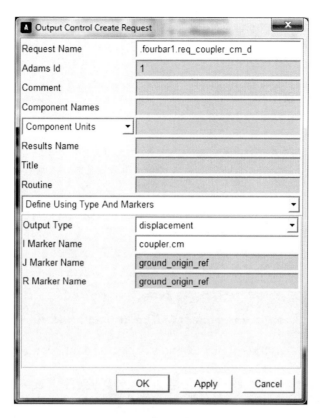

Figure 44 Coupler CM Displacement Request

The figure below uses traces to reveal the paths of the coupler center of mass marker and joint centers.

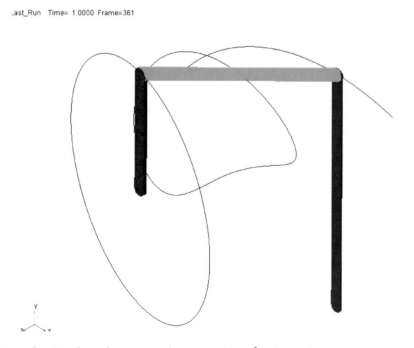

Figure 45 Coupler CM & End Trace Paths -- Fourbar → Skewed Driver and Non-Redundant Constraints

The figure below gives the displacement history of the coupler CM with respect to the ground reference marker.

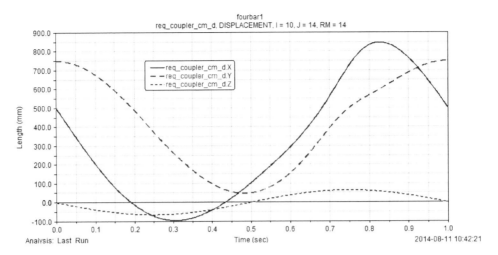

Figure 46 Coupler CM Displacement History

From the plot, it can be seen that the coupler CM now oscillates approximately 65 mm out-of-plane at 1 Hz.

Further Experimentation

The motivated reader may want to try some further modifications to this model. Suggested changes are:

1) Add gravity in the negative Y-direction. Does the system motion change? Hint: It had better not! In a 0 DOF model, the constraints determine all the motion, regardless of any applied loads.
2) Deactivate the driver motion. How many DOFs does the system now have? Execute it. Does it do anything? Hint: if it doesn't, what does that tell us about the equilibrium of the system's starting position?
3) Modify the initial conditions of the driver to give its CM an initial velocity of 1 mm/sec in the global X-direction. Does it move now? Hint: You may have to increase the end time of the simulation and up the number of output steps. Does the model behave as expected? Is energy conserved through the simulation? What happens if the solver error is tightened by a factor of, say, 10?
4) Using the default settings, add Coulombic ("sliding only") friction force to the driver/ground revolute joint. For "input forces to friction," specify "reaction force" only. How does the time behavior of the system change?

Example 2 -- Backhoe Excavator

Adams Features Employed in this Model:

1) **Fixed Joint**
2) **Revolute Joint**
3) **Spherical Joint**
4) **Translational Joint**
5) **Joint Primitive (INLINE)**
6) **Motion Constraint (Translational)**
7) **Motion Constraint (Rotational)**
8) **Design Variables**
9) **Gravity**
10) **Single Component Force, Action/Reaction, Translational (SFORCE)**
11) **Vector Force (VFORCE)**
12) **Generalized Force (GFORCE)**
13) **Differential State Variable (DIFF)**
14) **Output data requests**
15) **Sensors**

In this example, a backhoe excavator model (figure below) will be employed to determine the boom loads encountered during a dig/lift/swing/dump duty cycle operation. The model will initially be considered perfectly rigid, and then the boom structure will be rendered flexible, and the load cycle analysis will be repeated.

Comments on System Locations

As indicated in the theory section above, all locations of interest in an Adams model are specified with respect to the reference frame of the part to which they belong. Thus, if one is building a model of a system for which no assembled representation is available, but for which component representations are available, the components can be locally modeled by referring to position locations to the part reference (i.e., the "local part reference frame" → LPRF) and then locating the LPRFs (correctly) with respect to the system (Global) origin. This generally results in appreciable extra effort and is often a source of confusion to the modeler. For this excavator model, we will assume we are working, in effect, from an assembly drawing. Thus, all the part LPRFs will initially start off coincident and co-oriented with the Global origin and will initially have a QG vector of {0,0,0}. If a part moves, its QG vector and Euler orientation will become non-zero as the system articulates.

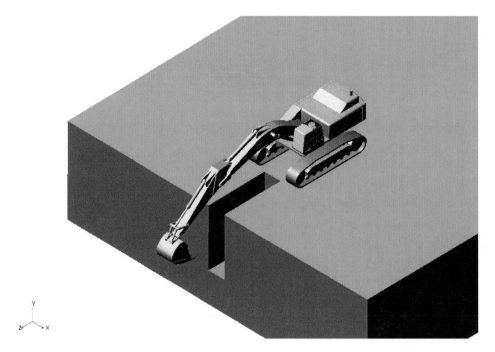

Figure 47 Idealized Excavator Model (Starting Position)

The variation of modeling elements during solution and the reasons for them will be detailed, as will the free-body equilibrium of the boom.

Model Components

The model idealization consists of the following, primary, components:

1) Undercarriage (crawler unit)
2) House (platform)
3) Boom
4) Dipper Stick
5) Bucket
6) Lift Cylinder assemblies (Quantity 2)
7) Crowd Cylinder assembly (dipper stick drive)
8) Cutting Cylinder assembly (bucket drive)
9) Bucket Linkage

Mass and CG data are provided below.

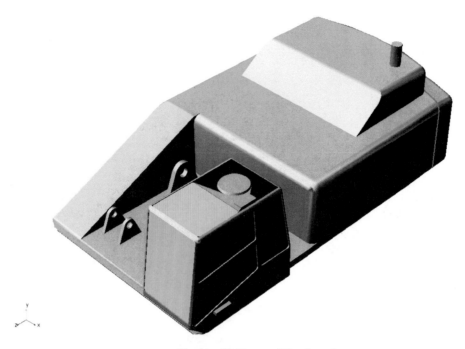

Figure 48 House (Platform)

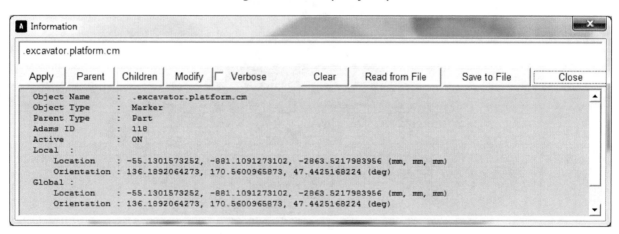

Figure 49 Platform Center-of-Mass Location & Orientation

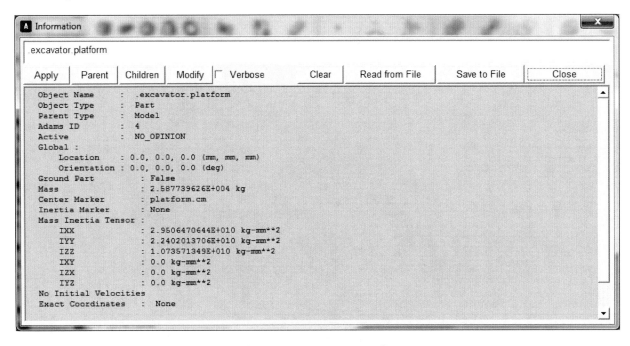

Figure 50 House Properties

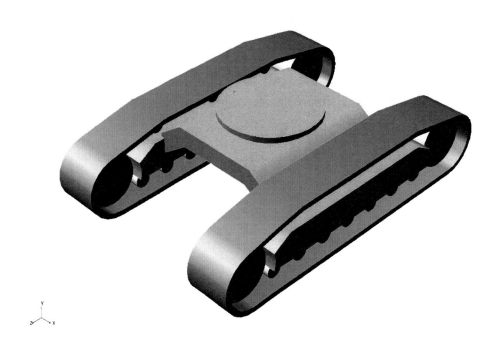

Figure 51 Crawler Assembly

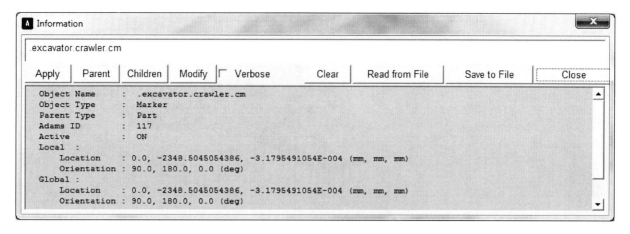

Figure 52 Crawler Center-of-Mass Location & Orientation

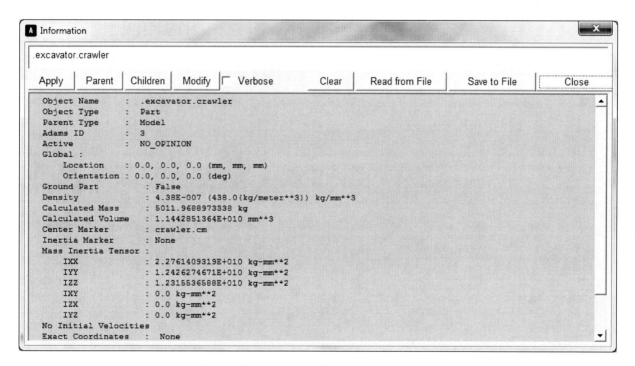

Figure 53 Crawler Properties

Figure 54 Boom

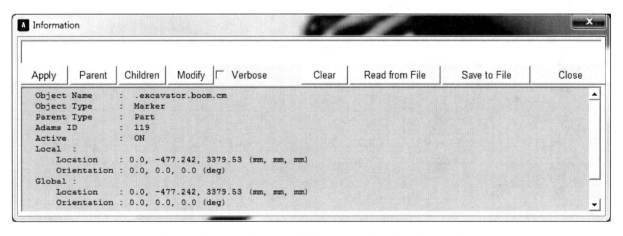

Figure 55 Boom Center-of-Mass Location & Orientation

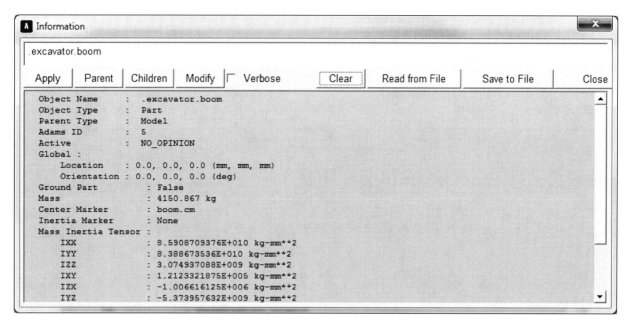

Figure 56 Boom Properties

Figure 57 Dipper

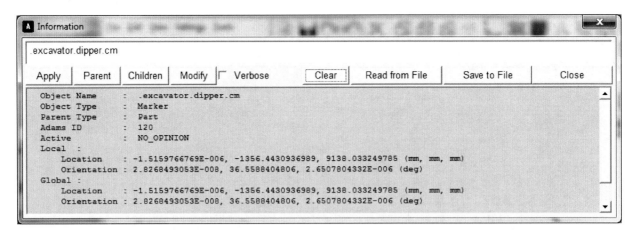

Figure 58 Dipper Center-of-Mass Location & Orientation

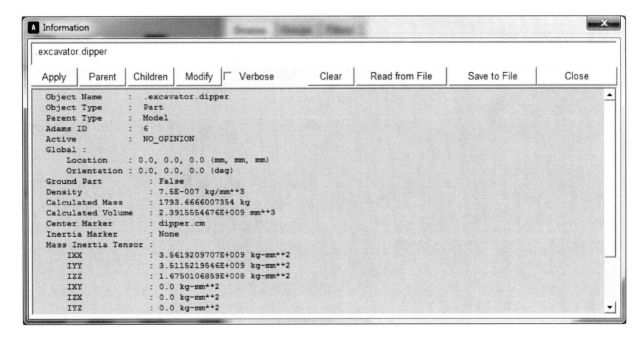

Figure 59 Dipper Properties

Figure 60 Bucket

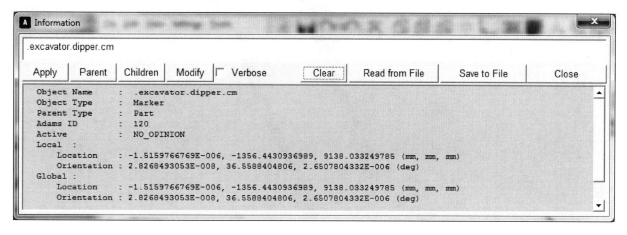

Figure 61 Bucket Center-of-Mass Location & Orientation

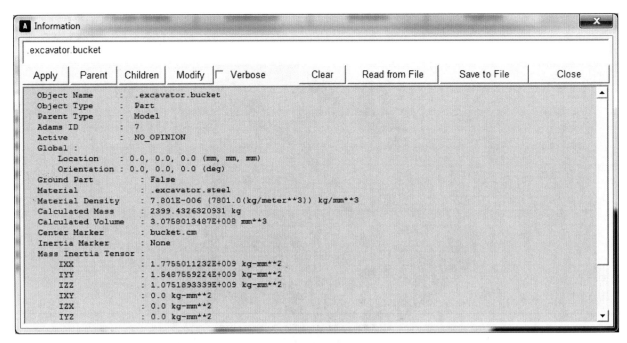

Figure 62 Bucket Properties

Figure 63 Bucket Links

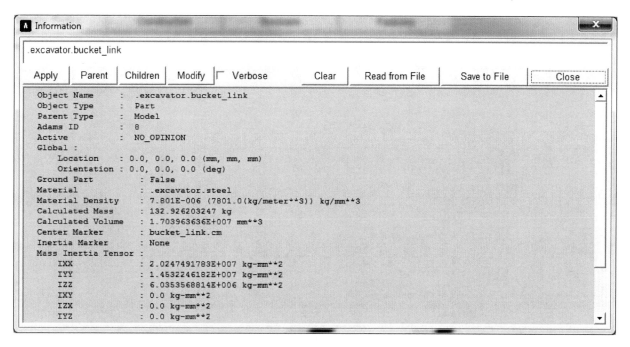

Figure 64 Bucket Link Properties

Figure 65 Arm Links

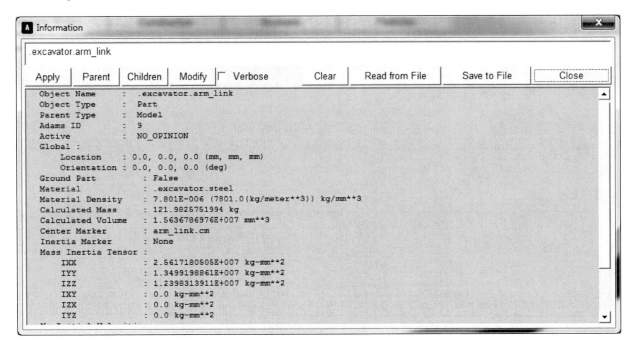

Figure 66 Arm Link Properties

Figure 67 Boom Cylinder Barrel (Left) -- Typical (Quantity 2)

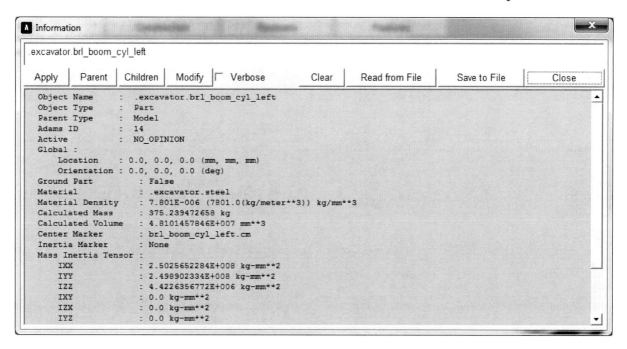

```
A  Information                                                                    x

.excavator.brl_boom_cyl_left

 Apply  |  Parent  |  Children  |  Modify  | ⌐ Verbose      Clear  |  Read from File  |  Save to File  |  Close

   Object Name      :   .excavator.brl_boom_cyl_left                                    ▲
   Object Type      :   Part
   Parent Type      :   Model
   Adams ID         :   14
   Active           :   NO_OPINION
   Global :
       Location     : 0.0, 0.0, 0.0  (mm, mm, mm)
       Orientation  : 0.0, 0.0, 0.0  (deg)
   Ground Part        : False
   Material           : .excavator.steel
   Material Density   : 7.801E-006 (7801.0(kg/meter**3)) kg/mm**3
   Calculated Mass    : 375.239472658 kg
   Calculated Volume  : 4.8101457846E+007 mm**3
   Center Marker      : brl_boom_cyl_left.cm
   Inertia Marker     : None
   Mass Inertia Tensor :
       IXX            : 2.5025652284E+008  kg-mm**2
       IYY            : 2.498902334E+008   kg-mm**2
       IZZ            : 4.4226356772E+006  kg-mm**2
       IXY            : 0.0 kg-mm**2
       IZX            : 0.0 kg-mm**2
       IYZ            : 0.0 kg-mm**2                                                    ▼
```

Figure 68 Boom Cylinder Barrel Properties

y
z   x

Figure 69 Boom Cylinder Rod (Left) -- Typical -- (Quantity 2)

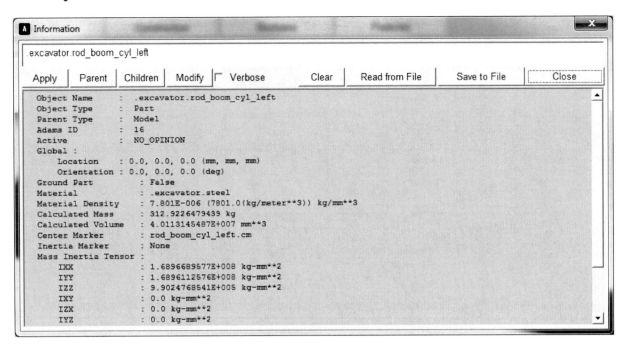

Object Name   : .excavator.rod_boom_cyl_left
Object Type   : Part
Parent Type   : Model
Adams ID   : 16
Active   : NO_OPINION
Global :
    Location   : 0.0, 0.0, 0.0 (mm, mm, mm)
    Orientation : 0.0, 0.0, 0.0 (deg)
Ground Part   : False
Material   : .excavator.steel
Material Density   : 7.801E-006 (7801.0(kg/meter**3)) kg/mm**3
Calculated Mass   : 312.9226479439 kg
Calculated Volume   : 4.0113145487E+007 mm**3
Center Marker   : rod_boom_cyl_left.cm
Inertia Marker   : None
Mass Inertia Tensor :
    IXX   : 1.6896689577E+008 kg-mm**2
    IYY   : 1.6896112576E+008 kg-mm**2
    IZZ   : 9.9024768541E+005 kg-mm**2
    IXY   : 0.0 kg-mm**2
    IZX   : 0.0 kg-mm**2
    IYZ   : 0.0 kg-mm**2

Figure 70 Boom Cylinder Rod Properties

Figure 71 Dipper Cylinder Barrel

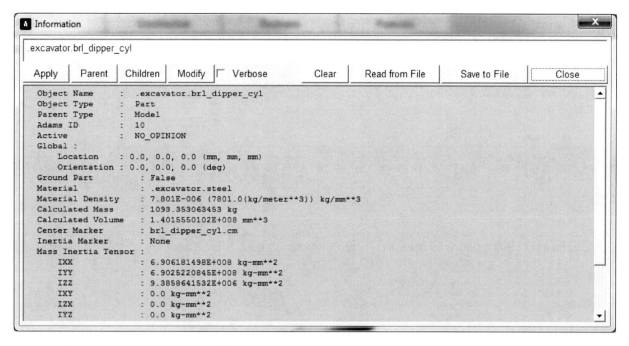

Figure 72 Dipper Cylinder Barrel Properties

Figure 73 Dipper Cylinder Rod

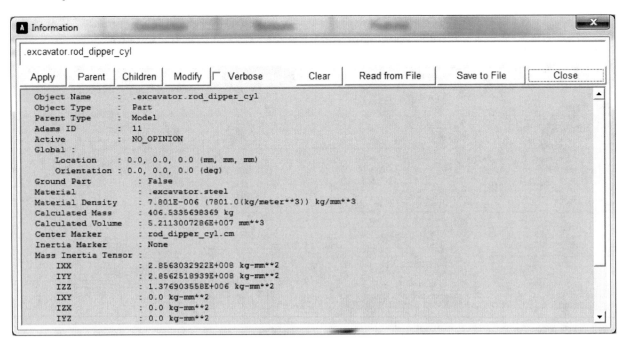

Figure 74 Dipper Cylinder Rod Properties

Figure 75 Bucket Cylinder Barrel

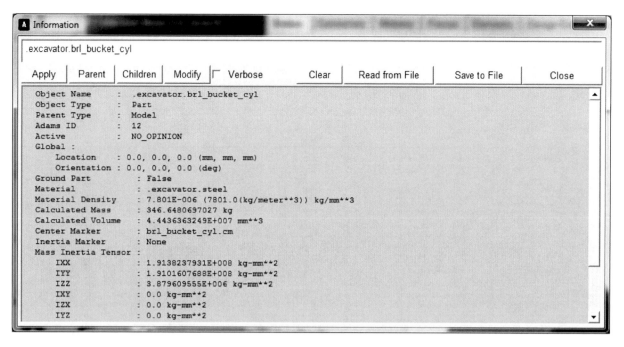

Figure 76 Bucket Cylinder Barrel Properties

Figure 77 Bucket Cylinder Rod

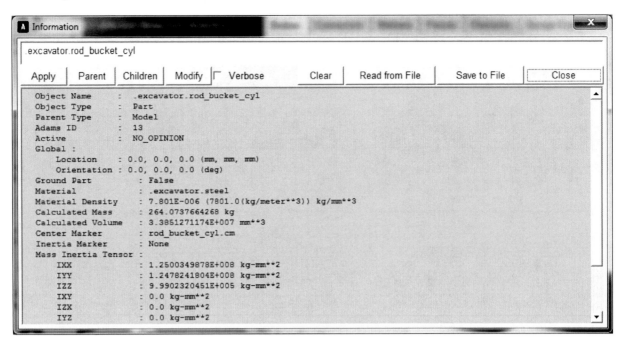

Figure 78 Bucket Rod Properties

The "DIRT" part is shown below. It represents, perhaps, the most contrived element in the model in that it attempts to represent the infinitely-variable bucket contents as a single, *un-deforming* part. However, as will be shown, it is possible to capture, at least approximately, the primary effect of the mass increase with time as the bucket fills.

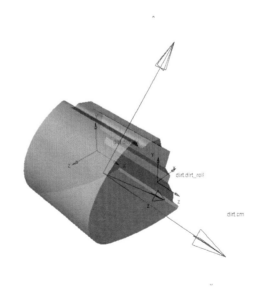

Figure 79 Dirt

The nominal mass properties of the DIRT are supplied in the bucket force modeling section below.

Total Model Aggregate Mass Computation

A very handy, as well as powerful, capability exists in Adams/View of computing the aggregate mass properties of an entire model in its initial (input) positions. The figure below shows this computation for the starting position of the excavator model.

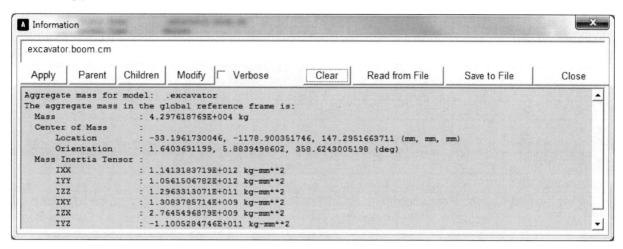

Figure 80 Aggregate (Total) Mass

It should be emphasized that this computation is only meaningful if the configuration itself is meaningful. Thus, if the initial assembly stages of the solution result in appreciable change in part positioning, an aggregate mass computation based on input positions may be meaningless. This potential problem can always be overcome by using the Adams/View model save capability to write out a new model version *after* initial assembly has taken place.

For the excavator model described here, the starting component positions of the dynamics analyses are very close to the input positions, making the information in figure 80 quite useful. For example, it has been used to ensure that the starting CG position of the excavator does, indeed, lie reasonably within the support area defined by the crawlers.

Model Connectivity (Gruebler Count)

The concept of the Gruebler count was introduced in the theory section and Adams pendulum model detailed above. For the sake of consistency, the Gruebler count of the excavator model will be determined in some detail. The model connections are tabularized below.

I_PART	J_PART	CONSTRAINT	DOFs	Remarks
Crawler	Ground	FIX Joint	-6	Anchor to ground
Platform	Crawler	REVOLUTE Joint	-5	
		MOTION	-1	
Boom	Platform	SPHERICAL Joint	-3	Reactions split to
		INLINE Jprim	-2	pin ends (See note 1)

Boom Cyl Brrl (r)	Platform	REVOLUTE Joint	-5	
Boom Cyl Brrl (l)	Platform	REVOLUTE Joint	-5	
Boom Cyl Rod (r)	Boom Cyl Brrl (r)	TRANSLATION Joint	-5	
Boom Cyl Rod (l)	Boom Cyl Brrl (l)	TRANSLATION Joint	-5	(Asymmetric drive for rigid model -- See note 2.)
		MOTION	-1	
Boom Cyl Rod (r)	Boom	INLINE Jprim	-2	
Boom Cyl Rod (l)	Boom	INLINE Jprim	-2	
Dipper Cyl Brrl	Boom	REVOLUTE Joint	-5	
Dipper Cyl Rod	Dipper Cyl Brrl	TRANSLATION Joint	-5	(See note 3)
		MOTION	-1	
Dipper Cyl Rod	Dipper	INLINE Jprim	-2	
Boom	Dipper	SPHERICAL Joint	-3	Reactions split to pin ends (See note 1)
		INLINE Jprim	-2	
Bucket Cyl Brrl	Boom	REVOLUTE Joint	-5	
Bucket Cyl Rod	Bucket Cyl Brrl	TRANSLATION Joint	-5	(See Note 4)
		MOTION	-1	
Bucket Cyl Rod	Dipper Links	INLINE Jprim	-2	
Dipper Links	Dipper	REVOLUTE Joint	-5	(Centered – See note 5)
Bucket Cyl Rod	Bucket Links	INLINE Jprim	-2	
Bucket	Dipper	REVOLUTE Joint	-5	
Bucket	Bucket Links	REVOLUTE Joint	-5	

Notes:

1) It has probably occurred to the reader that the boom/platform connection could also be accomplished with a single revolute joint, which would result in some model simplification while permitting the same single DOF of motion between the connected parts. This would be perfectly valid, as long as the parts continue to be modeled as rigid. However, this scenario will change when one (or both) of the connected parts is flexible, in which case it is desirable that the attachments be correctly located spatially. This issue will occur again at other locations in the model.

2) The left boom cylinder rod is constrained to move relative to left boom cylinder barrel by a single DOF, translational, time-dependent, motion constraint. It uses an Adams STEP function to hold the rod stroke at 0 until simulation time t = 5 seconds, at which point it is smoothly extended 500mm over 5 seconds. It should be noted that this represents, in effect, an open-loop control on the system. It should be further noted that, as long as the boom is modeled as rigid, any attempt to simultaneously place a similar constraint on the right boom cylinder would result in a conflicting, "redundant," constraint on the system. As a rule, constraint redundancies should always be avoided.

3) The dipper cylinder actuation motion provides a single DOF translational constraint on the dipper cylinder rod. Starting at time t = 0, it extends the dipper cylinder rod 1750 mm over 10 seconds, holds for 5 seconds, then retracts 1500 mm over 5 seconds. Like the left boom cylinder actuation, this represents an open-loop control on the system.

4) A translational motion constraint controls the bucket cylinder rod extension. Starting at time t=0, it extends 200 mm over 10 seconds and starting at time t= 15 seconds, retracts 800 mm over 4 seconds. This is also an open-loop control on the system.

5) From figures 63 and 65, it is clear that Adams (rigid) part definitions need not be contiguous. Further, constraints can be defined anywhere with respect to a part, even in "midair," if desired. What is important is that any mass properties, CG locations, and constraint definitions are spatially correct.

Invoking the Model Verify command within Adams/View, Adams will generate the basic statistics of the model.

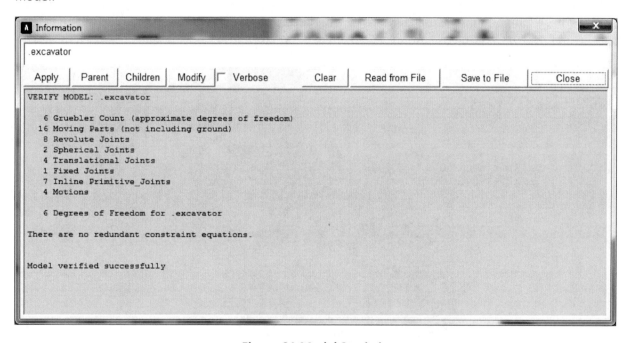

Figure 81 Model Statistics

It is worthwhile to delve a little deeper into these statistics.

The total DOF count introduced by the parts is:

60)

$$DOF = (17 - 1) * 6 = \ +96$$

The DOFs removed by the constraints are:

61)

$$DOF_{revolutes} = 8 * -5 = -40$$

$$DOF_{sphericals} = 2 * -3 = -6$$

$$DOF_{translationals} = 4 * -5 = -20$$

$$DOF_{fixed} = 1 * -6 = -6$$

$$DOF_{inlines} = 7 * -2 = -14$$

$$DOF_{motions} = 4 * -1 = -4$$

Summing the DOFs removed by the constraints, the total is -90. Thus, the excavator model, in its current, rigid configuration, has only 6 DOFs. These are associated with the DIRT part, which is temporarily restrained to the bucket by forces only. Furthermore, as will be detailed below, even these 6 DOFs will be temporarily constrained out of the model by a fixed joint between the DIRT and the bucket, and they will only be re-introduced when the bucket is ready to be emptied at the end of the cycle.

Bucket Load Modeling

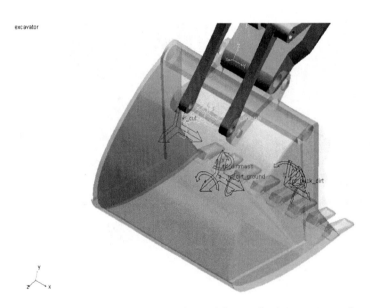

Figure 82 Bucket with Applied Force Locations

The dynamic forces experienced by an excavator bucket during a digging cycle are extremely complex. They generally include soil mechanics effects associated with material penetration, aggregate mass accumulation, contents shift with bucket attitude, transport, and dumping. Heavy equipment manufacturers have developed complex computer programs to determine these forces and apply them to their Adams models. For the model presented here, the bucket force modeling, while highly simplified, will nonetheless simulate:

1) Path-dependent cutting forces
2) Mass accretion associated with filling bucket contents
3) Bucket emptying

Bucket Cutting Forces

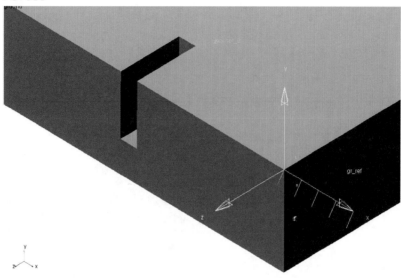

Figure 83 Ground with Cut "Trench" and Ground Reference MARKER "gr_ref"

The cutting force will be defined as a viscous (i.e., velocity-dependent), 3-component vector force (VFORCE "**vf_cut**") defined using the (globally-referenced) Z- (fore/aft) and Y-(vertical) velocities. This force will be shifted off-center to the right wall of the bucket and will take the form:

62)

$$F_y = -C_{cut} * V_y(i,j,r) * Step(dy(i,j,r), -500,1,1,0) * Step(dz(i,j,r), 0,1,500,0)$$

$$F_z = -C_{cut} * V_z(i,j,r) * Step(dy(i,j,r), -500,1,1,0) * Step(dz(i,j,r), 0,1,500,0)$$

Where,

F_y	→ the viscous force resisting Y-motion when the bucket is in the cut trench
F_z	→ the viscous force resisting Z-motion when the bucket is in the cut trench
C_{cut}	→ the coefficient of viscous resistance (25 N-sec/mm)
i,j,r	→ i is the tooth-centered marker on the bucket, j is the reference marker on ground, and r is the orientation marker, also on ground (the same marker as j).
Step(dy)	→ the vertical penetration of the trench top surface.
Step(dz)	→ the horizontal penetration of the trench vertical surface.

and,

Fx = 0.0

It should be noted that the cutting force components are not fully applied to the bucket wall marker until the bucket tooth marker has penetrated horizontally 500 mm into the trench face and are not fully zeroed until the bucket tooth marker has cleared the trench top surface by 500mm.

Bucket Load Mass Accretion

The "DIRT" part is shown in figure 79. Since any part possessing dynamical degrees of freedom must also possess corresponding mass/inertia properties, the "DIRT" part is given the small, token values shown below.

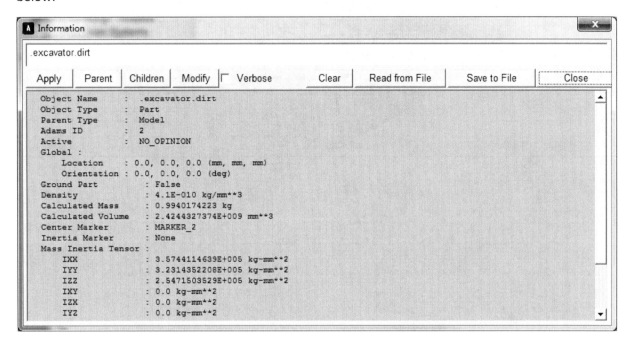

Figure 84 "DIRT" Token Mass and Inertias

As the dipper and boom cylinders stroke and the platform slews, the bucket cavity traverses a complex, 3-dimensional path. However, for the cutting phase, during which the accretion takes place, the bucket is practically limited to motion in the global XZ plane. A differential variable will be defined which computes the bucket reference point travel while the cut is taking place. It will be employed to accrete the bucket load proportionally with this travel.

The differential variable ("DIRT"), not to be confused with the part of the same name, will be defined as:

63)

$$\frac{d}{dt}DIRT = \left(SQRT\big(V_y(i,j,r) ** 2 + V_z(i,j,r) ** 2\big)\right) * STEPxON * STEPzON$$

...where the velocity terms are those defined for the cut force detailed above. The two, multiplying STEP functions serve to grow the DIRT term only when the bucket enters the trench. At this point, the model must be run to determine how long the DIRT path actually is, so this length can be used to scale the accretion factors for the load growth. It should be noted that, if the cylinder stroking is changed, this step must be repeated. Once this value (L_PATH) is known, the accretion in the mass (and, in similar fashion, the inertias) can be computed as

64)

$$m(t) = \frac{DIRT(t)}{L\_PATH} * m_{final}$$

According to Newton, the instantaneous force on a body is given by:

65)

$$\vec{F} = -\frac{d}{dt}(m\vec{v}) = -\frac{dm}{dt}\vec{v} - m\frac{d\vec{v}}{dt}$$

Thus, the Y- translational component of the mass accretion loading will be:

66)

$$Fy_{mass} = -\frac{\frac{d}{dt}DIRT}{L_{PATH}} * \frac{m_{final}}{G_c} * V_y(i,j,r) - \frac{DIRT}{L_{PATH}} * \frac{m_{final}}{G_c} * a_y(i,j,r) + G$$

Where...

$Mfinal$ → 3636 kg (assumed)
G_c → 1000 (units consistency constant due to mm length units)
A_y → DIRT part CG acceleration in the Y-direction
G → +9806.65 mm/sec^2

Note that gravity, acting in the negative Y (global) direction is modeled as a kinematic acceleration acting in the *plus* Y-direction. For the global X- and Z-directions, the translational mass accretion force will have the same form with the exception that the gravitational term (G) will drop away.

For the Y-inertial (i.e., angular) terms, the rotational inertia accretion torque will be
67)

$$Ty_{inertia} = -\frac{\frac{d}{dt}DIRT}{L_{PATH}} * \frac{Iy_{final}}{G_c} * \omega_y(i,j,r) - \frac{DIRT}{L_{PATH}} * \frac{Iy_{final}}{G_c} * \alpha_y(i,j,r)$$

Where...

$I_{y\ final}$ → 1.182e9 kg-mm^2
$_y$ →DIRT part CG angular velocity about the global Y-direction
$_y$ →DIRT part CG angular acceleration about the global Y-direction

For the global X- and Z-directions, the rotational inertial accretion torque will have the same form with the exception that $I_{x\ final}$=1.307e9 kg-mm^2 and $I_{z\ final}$= 9.318e8 kg-mm^2

Bucket Load Dump
The bucket load release force is a complete contrivance employed for graphical effects only.

Post-Dump DIRT-to-Ground force

The DIRT-to-ground GFORCE is also a complete modeling artifice employed for graphical effects only. Upon penetrating the ground XZ surface, massive (and completely fictitious) damping forces are ramped on to brake the DIRT, upon which inertial/gravitational forces are still acting, to a (near) halt.

Model Variation During Execution Using the Adams (ACF) Command File

An Adams command file (ACF, also called a "simulation script" within Adams/View) is primarily used to set the program execution parameters during an Adams simulation. However, it also contains the very powerful capability of altering the Adams model itself during execution by employing activate/deactivate commands at various stages of the solution. For the bucket load release described above, the "DIRT" part was rigidly locked to the bucket by a fixed joint for most of the action cycle. Since, as explained above, the forces between the DIRT and bucket are highly contrived, nothing would be gained by trying to accurately define the complex nature of the contact between these two parts. It is, however, desirable to permit the DIRT to separate from the bucket in a somewhat realistic fashion, if only for enhanced graphical effect. Thus, at the somewhat arbitrary simulation time of t = 19 sec, the fixed joint between the DIRT part and the bucket is deactivated. It should be cautioned that use of the deactivate command represents a basically *discontinuous* change to the model topology and there can be undesirable numerical consequences of employing this capability. One such consequence will be examined in the results reported below. The ACF file used for the rigid model is shown in the figure below.

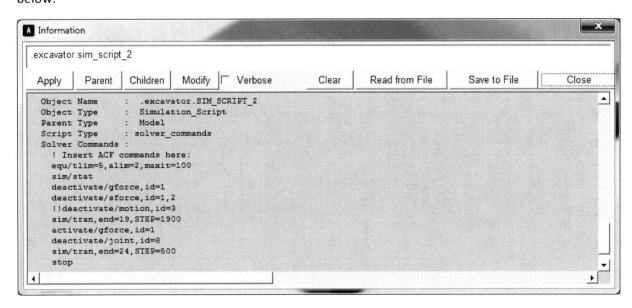

Figure 85 Excavator Model -- Rigid -- Adams ACF File

Briefly explained:

1) The **equ** command is employed to modify the static solution parameters from the default settings. **tlim** limits the maximum translational change of any part displacement to 5 mm for any iteration, **alim** limits the maximum rotational change of any part displacement to 2 radians, and **maxit** ups the maximum number of attempted iterations from the default of 25 to 100.

2) The **sim/stat** command instructs the solver to perform a static solution.

3) The **deactivate/gforce,id=1** command turns off the DIRT/bucket GFORCE while the DIRT/bucket fixed joint is active. Later in the simulation, when the DIRT is dumped, the force is turned back on simultaneously with the fix joint being turned off.

4) The **deactivate/sforce,id=1,2** command turns off the boom cylinder forces, which are over-ridden by the left boom cylinder motion constraint. These will be left active and the motion will be turned off when the boom is rendered flexible.

5) The **!!deactivate/motion,id=3** command, which strokes the left boom cylinder, is ignored because it is preceded by an exclamation mark (only one is needed), which turns the text into a comment. Later, when this ACF script is modified to run the model with the flexible boom, this command will be activated since the boom elevation is then controlled by twin, stroking boom cylinder SFORCEs.

Boom Reaction Force Reporting

The boom connection forces will all be reported using Adams output data request statements in the boom-fixed, red coordinate system triad (marker bm_piv_l) shown in the figure shown below.

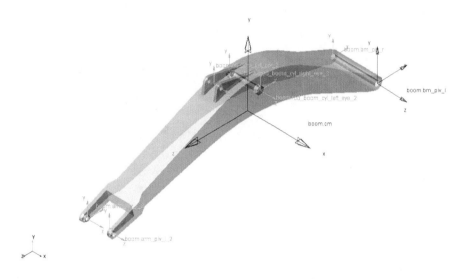

Figure 86 Boom Connection Force Reporting Orientation (Rigid Boom)

Conversion to Flexible Boom

An MSC Nastran model of the (simplified) boom structure was generated from the geometry shown in the figure above and then meshed.

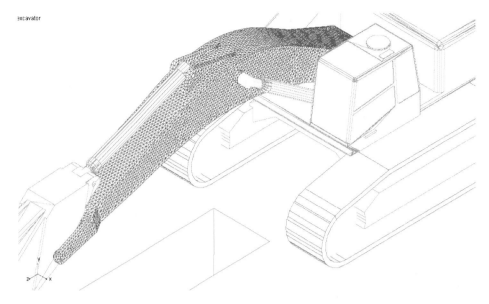

Figure 87 Flexible Boom Structure --Meshed & Installed (Hidden Line Graphic)

The structure material is steel and the elements employed are MSC Nastran CTETRA solid and CTRIA3 shell elements. The model is defined using 9850 MSC Nastran GRIDs.

Figure 88 Flexible Boom -- Structural Scheme

The internal bulkheads and vertical box webs are 5 mm plate, the upper box cap is 10 mm plate and the lower box cap is 7.5 mm plate. The darkened components in the figure are solid steel. The mass properties of the structure are given below.

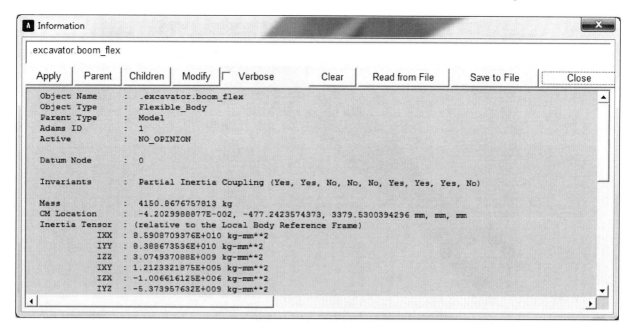

Figure 89 Flexible Boom Properties

Boom Structure Flex Content

The flexible content of an Adams FLEXBODY can come from 2 sources: Craig-Bampton ("hardpoint") freedoms and scalar freedoms. In MSC Nastran, the former are those freedoms associated with connection points for which precise (ASET1) stiffnesses are required. To acquire them, a Guyan reduction is executed on the structure. This extracts the hardpoint coefficient (sub-)matrices and also lumps the complete system mass onto the same hardpoints. In general, this gives a precise stiffness but a very poor mass representation of the structure. To rectify this, scalar modes are generated with the hardpoint freedoms fixed to ground. At this point, the structure coefficient matrices are comprised of mixed types. The hardpoint coefficient submatrices are Cartesian/aperiodic, while the scalar submatrices are modal/frequency-dependent. Consequently, a second eigenvalue analysis (known as an "orthonormalization") is performed on the mixed system, which converts the entire structure to the frequency domain.

The figures below display some of the boom structure eigenmodes for which the superposition of the deflected mode shape is superimposed on the un-deflected geometry.

ex Body=boom_flex Mode=7 (24.281930 Hz)

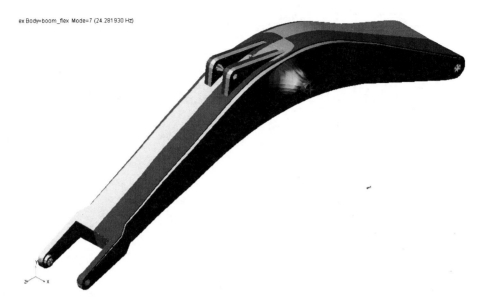

Figure 90 Flex Boom; 1st Structural Mode (Trunnion Lateral Shift @ 24+ Hz)

ex Body=boom_flex Mode=8 (29.465053 Hz)

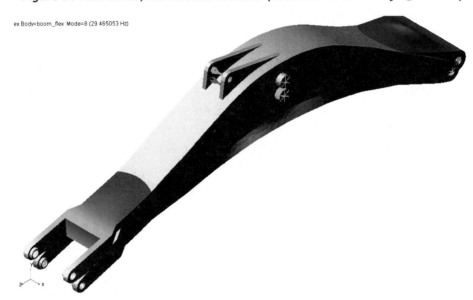

Figure 91 Mode 8 → 2nd Boom Structural Mode (Vertical Beam Bending @ 29+ Hz)

ex Body=boom_flex Mode=32 (95.263402 Hz)

Figure 92 Mode 32 -->26th Boom Structural Mode (Beam Torsion @ 95+ Hz)

The boom structure in this model has 7 attachment points with varying DOF connection freedoms. The right boom/platform connection has 3 constraints, while the left has 2 constraints. The boom cylinder attachments at the upper trunnion each possess 2 DOFs. The dipper cylinder barrel connection results in 5 DOFs for restraint, and the 2 dipper connections result in the need for a further 5 elastic DOFs. Thus, the *minimum*, total, boom attachment hardpoint DOF count is 19. If, however, any of the connection modeling to the boom Adams were to be changed, this would necessitate modification to the MSC Nastran model, followed by its (re-)execution. To be safe, All 6 DOFs at all the connection points to the boom are retained, thus 42 Craig-Bampton freedoms are generated, to which a further 24 scalar freedoms are added. The result is a flexibility count of 66 elastic DOFs. It should be noted that the first 6 of these freedoms provide the rigid body modes for the structure and will be near-zero in frequency, reducing the usable elastic DOF count for the boom to 60.

It is worthwhile to mention that the solver analysis time for a model with a FLEXBODY is independent of the MSC Nastran model mesh size and depends almost exclusively on the number of retained modes. Thus our 66 elastic DOF model would execute in Adams at the same speed even if the mesh were increased from 9000+ GRIDS to 9 *million* plus GRIDS while calling for, again, 66 elastic DOFs, and models with FLEXBODYs approaching this size are not uncommon. Such a large FEA model *would* cause difficulties if graphical animation were attempted in Adams/View. To circumvent this problem, MSC Nastran permits the use of graphical outline (PLOTEL) elements to reduce the graphical content of a FLEXBODY to a reasonable size.

Special Note: When employing FLEXBODYs in an Adams model, the question always arises: "How many elastic modes do I need?" The answer depends on two primary factors: accuracy of the connection stiffnesses and correctness of the model frequency content. The former is guaranteed if the FEA model GRIDs are "master" nodes defined in the MSC Nastran ASET1 specification. The latter depends on the highest frequency of interest in the model. The modal condensation employed in generating the structure MNF file usually begins to degrade at the half-way point up the frequency scale. Thus, as "a

rule of thumb," the highest active frequency in the model should be at least twice the highest frequency of interest.

Flexible/Rigid Results Comparison

The model is executed using Adams' GSTIFF, SI2 integrator for a total of 25 seconds in 2500 output steps. Since the system with the flexible boom remains unrealistically stiff because of its use of predominantly rigid elements, the proportional structural viscous damping (CRATIO) for the flexible boom is (arbitrarily) set to 50% of critical damping. The plots below compare forces acting on the excavator boom at selected connection points to the system.

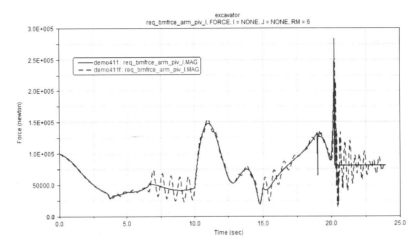

Figure 93 Comparison -- Left Boom/Dipper Pin Force Magnitude -- (Red Curve Rigid; Blue Curve Flex)

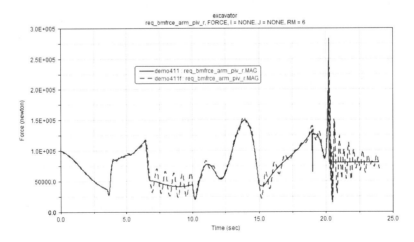

Figure 94 Comparison -- Right Boom/Dipper Pin Force Magnitude --- (Red Curve Rigid; Blue Curve Flex)

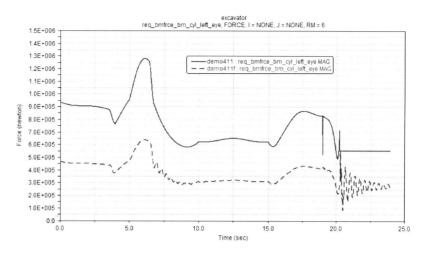

Figure 95 Comparison -- Left Boom/Boom Cylinder Attach Force Magnitude-- (Red Curve Rigid; Blue Curve Flex)

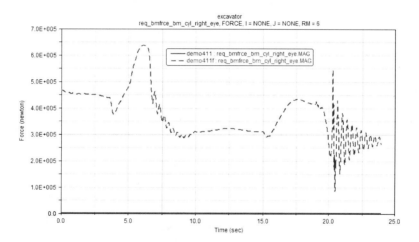

Figure 96 Comparison -- Right Boom/Boom Cylinder Attach Force Magnitude-- (Red Curve Rigid; Blue Curve Flex)

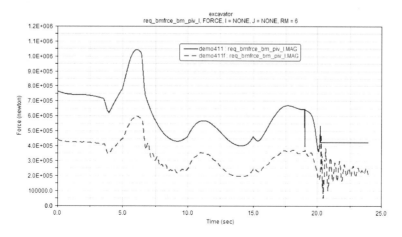

Figure 97 Comparison – Left Boom/Platform Pin Force Magnitude -- (Red Curve Rigid; Blue Curve Flex)

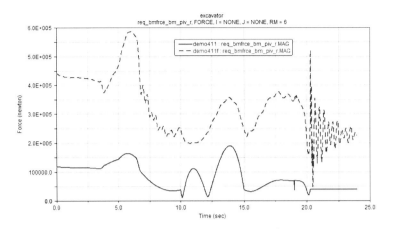

*Figure 98 Comparison – Right Boom/Platform Attach Force Mag*nitude - *(Red Curve Rigid; Blue Curve Flex)*

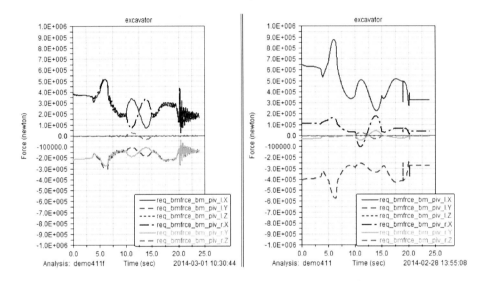

Figure 99 Boom/Platform Connection Force Distribution – Curves 1 → 3 Left Attach; Curves 4 → 6 Right Attach (Left Plot --> Flex Boom; Right Plot --> Rigid Boom)

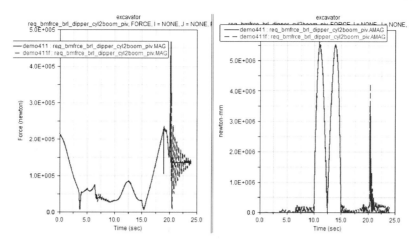

Figure 100 Comparison -- Dipper Cylinder/Boom Attach Forces/Moments – Magnitudes (Red Curves Rigid; Blue Curves Flex)

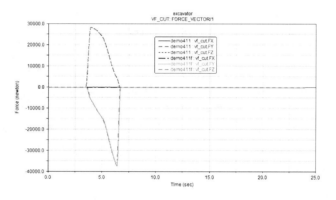

Figure 101 Comparison -- Bucket Cut Forces (Curves 1 --> 3 Rigid; Curves 4-->6 Flex)

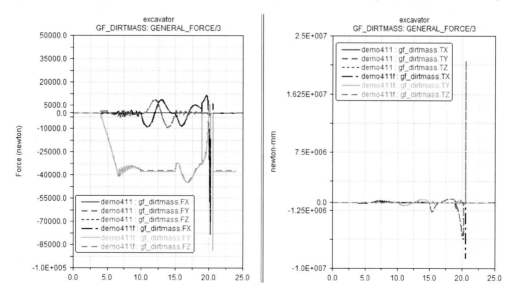

Figure 102 Comparison -- Mass Accretion ('DIRT') Forces & Torques (Curves 1 --> 3 Rigid; Curves 4 -->6 Flex)

Excavator Results – Comments

From the curves above it is clear that representing the boom as flexible has resulted in significant changes to the forces connecting it. Specifically:

1) All force comparison traces now contain the oscillatory signature of the flexible boom.
2) The cutting force (figure 100) is virtually the same for both models.
3) At the start of the simulation, the rigid model has 0 DOFs. At simulation time t = 19 seconds, the fixed joint locking the DIRT part to the bucket is deactivated with a simulation script. This brings the DIRT/bucket GFORCE into play. At this point, the model has 6 DOFs.
4) At the start of the simulation, the flexible model has 61 DOFs. This results from the introduction of 60 elastic DOFs with the FLEXBODY and from the boom cylinder actuation motion constraint (1 DOF) being replaced by 2 coupled actuators (SFORCEs). When the DIRT/bucket fixed joint is deactivated, and the GFORCE comes into play, the model DOF count grows to 67 DOFs.
5) The de-activation of the fixed constraint locking the DIRT to the bucket results, not unexpectedly, in a sharp "spike" on the results for the rigid boom, but these spikes are absent, or, at least, greatly reduced on the flexible model.
6) While, except for the elastic oscillations of the flexible model, the dipper/boom loads (figures 93, 94) and dipper cylinder/boom loads (figure 100) are very similar, the boom/platform loads are substantially different between to two models (figures 97 through 99). This is to be expected, since the boom free-body equilibrium of the two models will be different due to the fact that the boom elevation is driven by the left cylinder *only* in the rigid model, but by *both* cylinders equally in the flexible model. Figure 99 shows the fundamental differences in the boom free-body forces. For the flexible model (with both boom cylinders stroking), the boom/platform attachment loads are almost equal, except during the platform slew. For the rigid model, however, since only the left cylinder is in play as an actuator, the boom/platform loads are quite different.
7) The force and moment components due to mass accretion to the DIRT part is given in figure 102. The "weight" of the dirt accumulated is approximately 37462 N. This corresponds to a mass of 3820 kg, which is within 5% of the assumed full value of the mass accreted to DIRT.

Possible Further Excavator Model Enhancements

As shown above, the addition of only one flexible component can significantly affect the performance of a mechanical system. The flexible rendering of all of the primary, articulating components could be accomplished in the same fashion as was done for the boom. Perhaps of at least equal significance would be the inclusion of power plant and hydraulic pump feedback effects. These would both have an effect on the stroking rates achieved by the cylinders driving the boom and, thus, the cycle times and the associated loads. Three possibilities are available:

1) Add the powerplant/pump effects directly to the excavator model using the available Adams modeling elements.
2) Couple the Adams excavator model to a separate controls model of the powerplant/hydraulic system. This could be done by executing the problem inside Adams while exporting plant information to the controls package and importing the cylinder forces from the controls package. Alternatively, it could be done executing the problem inside the controls package, while importing force and positional information from Adams.

3) Co-simulation is also possible. Both Adams and the controls model would run simultaneously using their own integrators, and a numeric-based "glue code" would manage the continuous data exchange between the programs.

While all three options are viable, option 2 is certainly the most straightforward and the easiest to implement.

Example 3 -- Automotive Differential (Adams/Machinery Model)

Adams Features Employed in this Model:

1) **The Adams/Machinery vertical application**
2) **The Gear User Defined Element (UDE)**
3) **Boolean operations on user-defined geometry**
4) **Contact force element**
5) **The user-defined constraint (UCON)**
6) **Evaluation/post-processing of results objects**

Note: a slightly simpler version of this model is available to the user in the Adams/Machinery Tutorial delivered with the Adams/Machinery product. The tutorial contains the complete, step-by-step inputs used to build the model, so, for the sake of brevity, the description of the build process will be kept to a minimum here and will concentrate primarily on differences with the tutorial version.

While Adams is general enough to create a model of almost any system definable in the Newtonian sense, the complexities associated with many engineering definitions of interest often make the custom generation of an Adams model to represent the problem so complex as to be impractical. Components such as gear sets, belt or chain drives, roller bearings, cable systems, and cams require minute detail to correctly capture the physics of interest. Fortunately, the Adams/View command language is sufficiently powerful to permit the creation of application-specific modeling environments (i.e., "vertical apps") of almost any degree of complexity. When fundamental, topologically-consistent, but dimensionally varying modeling elements are repeatedly needed, it becomes worthwhile to employ specialized, Adams/View-based modeling elements. A case in point is the generation of geared assemblies. This example performs a contact-based analysis of a loaded automotive differential in a vehicle executing a turn. The figure below shows the system of interest.

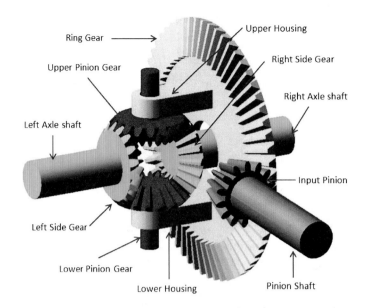

Figure 103 (Adams Machinery) Automotive Differential Model

Problem Definition

The model will be used to solve the following problem:

Given: A front-wheel drive vehicle with a track width of 2.3 meters is executing a left-hand turn for which the inside (left) wheel is describing a circular path of radius 4-meters, at a constant speed of 15 kilometers/hour. The vehicle mass is 1135 kg, the front/rear tire load distribution is 50%/50%, and the loaded tire rolling radius is 0.4 meters. The differential ring gear is located on the vehicle centerline. Assume the pavement is concrete and that load shift due to the centripetal acceleration of the turn can be ignored.

Determine: a) the driving torque which must be provided by the pinion gear to overcome the drive tire rolling resistance while propelling the vehicle through the turn; and **b)** the associated pinion/ring gear contact forces that result.

Determination of Wheel Loads

A speed of 15 kilometers/hour corresponds to a vehicular translational velocity in model units of:

68)

$$v_{mm/sec} = v_{km/hr} \times 1000_{m/km} \times 1000_{mm/m} \times \frac{1_{hr}}{3600_{sec}} = 4166.666_{mm/sec}$$

The nominal angular velocity of the tire required to achieve this speed is:

69)

$$\omega_{rad/sec} = \frac{v_{mm/sec}}{r_{mm}} = \frac{4166.666}{400.0} = 10.416_{rad/sec}$$

98

Note that the angular velocity value above (which is also 596.729 deg/sec) will also be the spin velocity of the differential ring gear.

However, because the vehicle is turning, the outside wheel will be rotating faster and the inside wheel will be rotating slower than the nominal angular velocity computed above. The path turn radii for the ring gears and wheels are:

Inside wheel →   R = 4 m (given)

Ring Gear →   R = 4 + Track/2 = 5.15 m

Outside wheel →   R = 4 + Track = 6.3 m

The angular velocity of each wheel can be computed from:

70)

$$\omega_{wheel} = R_{wheel}/R_{ring\_gear} \times \omega_{ring\_gear}$$

From the equation above, the angular velocity of the outboard wheel is 12.742 rad/sec (730.062 deg/sec), and the angular velocity of the inboard wheel is 8.080 rad/sec (462.949 deg/sec). Thus, during the turn, the outer wheel must turn 1.577 times faster than the inner wheel.

From [4, p.111], the rolling resistance wheel force is given by:

71)

$$R_x = f_r \times W$$

...where f_r is the rolling force coefficient and W is the vehicle weight. For a passenger car tire on concrete pavement, reference [4, p117] gives a value of f_r of 0.015. The total rolling resistance force is 166.958 N. Each tire drag force will be 166.958/4 (= 41.739N) acting at a 400 mm tire radius, resulting in a drag torque on each wheel of 16,695.821 Nmm.

The Differential Model Elements

This model is a derivative of the Adams/Machinery Tutorial problem as cited above, and, for the sake of simplification, is also constructed with the input pinion, ring gear, and axle shafts grounded. This removes the need to include the dynamics of the vehicle motion with respect to ground, although this could certainly be done. This means that the axle shaft motions and applied torques will have to be supplied to the problem.

The UDE Gear Set

The **U**ser-**D**efined-**E**lement (UDE) is a pre-defined, high-level modeling element which, in general, contains a substantial amount of application-specific data. As such, it can automatically generate a tremendous amount of information. There is, however, a price to pay in terms of some lost generality for the benefit of this utility. More about this later.

The gears and their properties are given in the table below.

ID	# Teeth	Pressure Angle (deg)	Tooth ISO #	Pitch Angle (deg)	Pitch Apex (deg)	Face Width (mm)	Back Dist (mm)	Profile Shift Coef	Add-endum Factor	Ded-endum Factor	Thk Mod Coef	Shaft D (mm)	Bore R (mm)
Ring	60	20.0	23509	76.865	0.0	40.0	0.0	-0.505	1.0	1.25	-0.055	na	25.0
Pinion	14	20.0	23509	13.134	0.0	40.0	0.0	+0.505	1.0	1.25	0.037	10.0	na
L Drive	18	20.0	23509	45.0	0.0	25.4	0.0	-0.505	1.0	1.25	-0.055	20.0	na
R Drive	18	20.0	23509	45.0	0.0	25.4	0.0	-0.505	1.0	1.25	-0.055	20.0	na
U Spdr	18	20.0	23509	45.0	0.0	25.4	0.0	0.505	1.0	1.25	0.037	10.0	na
L Spdr	18	20.0	23509	45.0	0.0	25.4	0.0	0.505	1.0	1.25	0.037	10.0	na

Table 5 – Differential Gear Properties

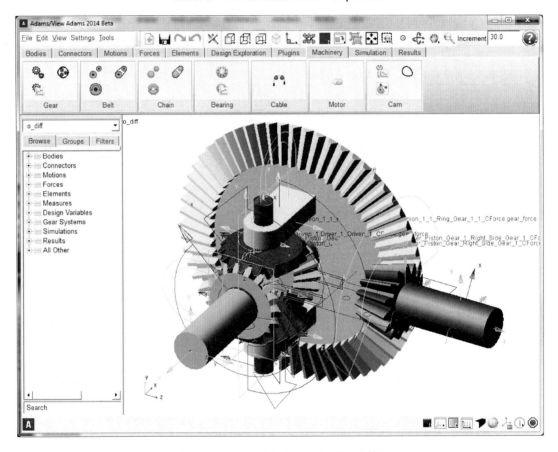

Figure 104 Finished Model "o-diff"

In figure 104 above, **Machinery** has been selected from the menu ribbon, causing an array of machinery-based build options to appear. Since it is highly repetitive, detailed explanation of the gear build process will be limited to the drive pinion and ring gear interaction.

As a first step, **Points** are specified in ground at important locations such as those defining gear centers, shaft axes, etc. These are used to locate and orient the differential components during construction.

POINT ID	X	Y	Z	Purpose
A	-45	0	0	Locate left side gear

B	45	0	0	Locate right side gear
C	0	43	0	Locate upper pinion gear
D	0	-43	0	Locate lower pinion gear
E	40	0	137	Locate Ring Gear
F	0	50	0	Locate Right Side Gear
G	0	-50	0	Locate Left Side Gear
H	40	0	200	Locate Input Pinion Gear

Table 6 – Differential Design Points

The arrangement of the design points in ground is shown below.

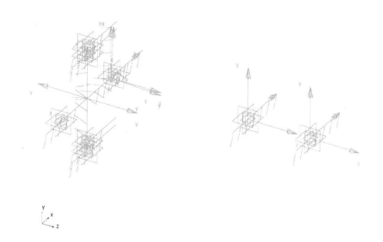

Figure 105 Point Locations (Ground)

Once the points are available, the gears are specified in sets of 2 using them. The six step procedure is shown below.

Step 1 defines the type of gear to be built. There are 6 options:

1) Spur
2) Helical
3) Bevel
4) Worm
5) Rack
6) Hypoid

Since all of the differential gears are bevel gears, it is selected.

Figure 106 Bevel Gear Build Option -- Step 1

Step 2 (Method) determines how the gearing is defined. Two options, "Simplified" and "3D Contact" are possible. The former generates a simplified elastic restraint relationship between the spin freedoms of the two gear parts, while the latter actually generates forces based on the instantaneous volume intersections of the geometry defining the gear bodies. More detail on the generation of these forces is provided below.

Figure 107 Gear Geometry Definition (Input Pinion/Ring Gear Set) -- Step 3

Figure 108 Gear Material and Contact Property Specifications -- Step 4

Note that input must be entered for ***both*** gears.

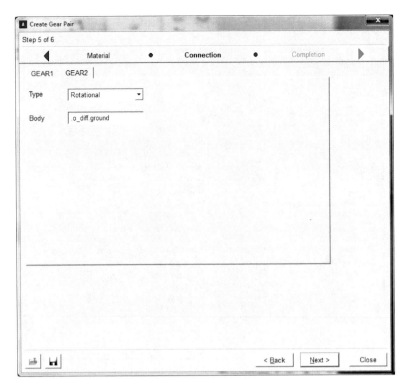

Figure 109 Gear Set Interaction Definition -- Step 5

Note that, again, input must be entered for **both** gears.

Figure 110 Gear Definition Finish -- Step 6

To provide some idea as to the effort that has been saved by employing the gear UDE, let us examine the physical data for the gear set just generated using the model browser.

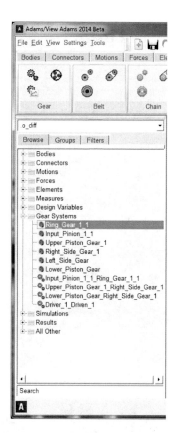

Figure 111 Gear Systems Accessed from the Model Browser – Ring Gear

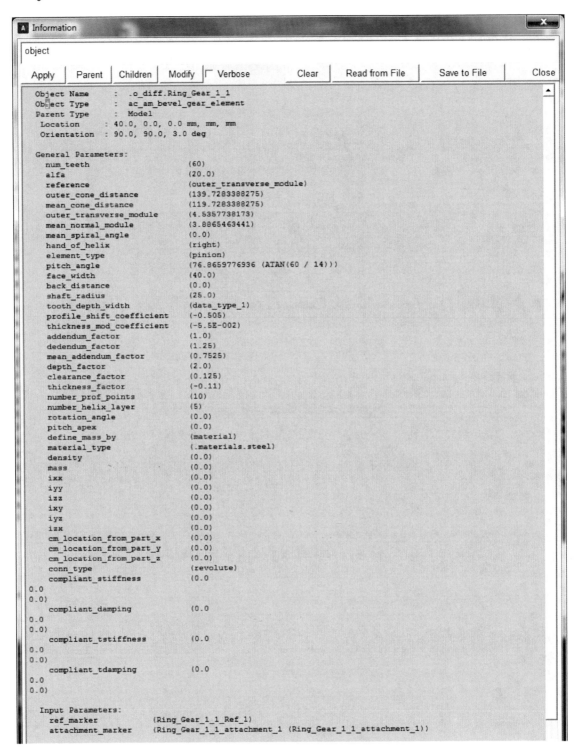

Figure 112 UDE Definition of 60 Tooth, Beveled, Ring Gear

The same type of information is auto-generated for the associated pinion gear.

Using the model browser again, the gear set definition is examined.

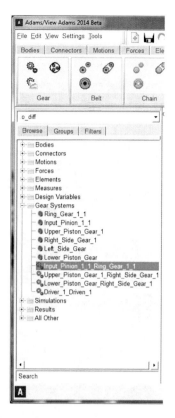

Figure 113 Gear Systems Accessed from the Model Browser – Pinion/Ring Gear Force Definition

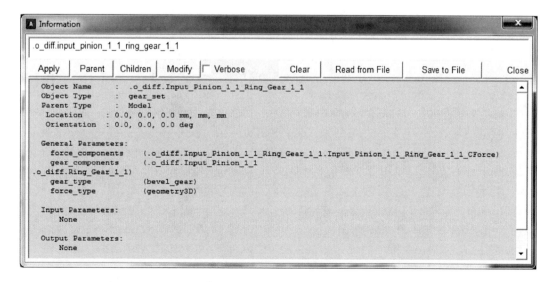

Figure 114 Pinion/Ring Gear Force Component Identification

Some UDE Considerations

As was mentioned above, there is a small price to be paid for the utility gained using, in this case, the gear set generator. Because of the defining parameterization of the gear geometries needed for the complex tooth geometries, the definitions of the gear parts are limited and cannot be directly extended. For example, the figure below shows the ring gear part created by the UDE.

gear_part

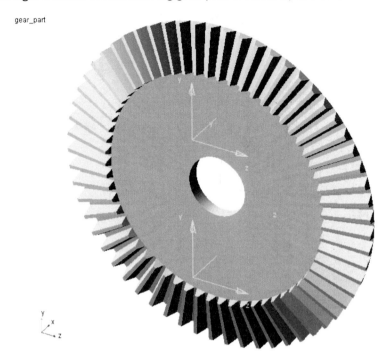

Figure 115 UDE-Generated Ring Gear Part

While the GEAR UDE does permit cylindrical shafts to be added, or cylindrical shaft bores to be cut into the defined gear body geometry along their spin axes, more general additions, such as those required for the two ring gear "housings" necessary to attach the upper and lower pinion gears, are not permitted, since this would require a Boolean solid addition operation between the geometries which would change (hence, corrupt) the already-defined (and greatly detailed) gear geometry. To permit the inclusion of such necessary components, the additions are defined as separate parts and then locked to the UDE-defined part (refer to figure 104) with fixed joints which do not affect the geometric definition of the gear. While this adds equations to the system, unless hundreds of such custom gear parts are needed, it should not be a problem. However, before the housings can be locked to the ring gear, they must be created. Prior to constructing the housing solids, the shafts will be added to the gears so that they can be used to define the bores for the upper and lower pinion gears. The gear shafts are added to the gear geometry using the Adams/View command sequence:

108

Bodies/RigidBody:Cylinder/

Add to **Part/Length**(*enter length*)**/ Radius**(*enter radius*)**/**

(Right_Side_Gear/(*orient cylinder axis using click & drag*)

A shaft 40 mm in diameter and 100 mm long is added to the right side gear. Using these same dimensions, shafts are added to the left side gear and the input pinion. Using the same sequence, shafts 20 mm in diameter and 50 mm long are added to the upper and lower pinion gears.

Bodies/RigidBody:Box/

New Part/Length(*enter 70 mm*)**/ Height**(*enter 20 mm*)**/Depth**(*enter 40 mm*)

Pick Corner/(*click point F*)

The steps above cause a new part with a default name of PART_# to be created. Rename this part "Upper_Housing." From the Main Toolbox, right click **Position:Reposition objects**

Select Position:move/Selected/Vector method

/Distance → 20mm/(*define the* *direction vector in the negative-Z direction using the box* *geometry*)

At this point, a cylinder 20 mm long, with a 20 mm radius, and centers using point C is added to the re-positioned box.

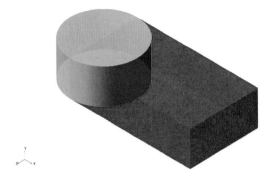

Figure 116 Intersecting Geometric Primitives (Block and Cylinder) – Upper Housing

The block and cylinder are next merged into a single "Constructive_Solid_Geometry" (CSG) entity by performing a Boolean addition.

This results in...

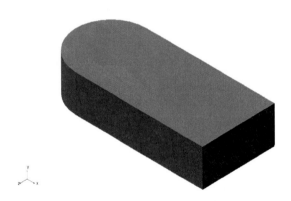

Figure 117 Intermediate Upper_Housing CSG Solid

This is followed by a Boolean subtraction using the upper pinion gear shaft cylinder to "cut" the intermediate CSG solid.

This results in the finalized geometry.

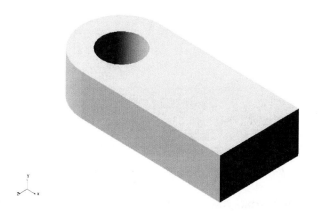

Figure 118 Final Upper_Housing CSG Solid

By right-clicking on the Upper_Housing part and selecting **Modify/Mass Properties**, its material can be declared as "steel," resulting in its CG, mass, and inertial values being computed using the CSG properties. The same procedures above could be repeated to generate the Lower_Housing part. But that is not necessary. The Upper_Housing part can simply be copied, moved down 120 mm and re-named Lower_Housing.

Mechanism Constraints – Intrinsic

Adams/Machinery creates a revolute joint for each grounded shaft, removing a total of 20 DOFs from the system. Two fixed joints must be added to secure the housing assemblies to the ring gear. These remove another 12 DOFs from the system.

Although the upper and lower pinion gears have been created, they have not yet been constrained to the system because their connecting geometry did not yet exist. Now that the shaft bores on the housings exist, revolute joints, bore-centered on the housings can be created, removing another 10 DOFs.

The differential is driven by a motion constraint on the input pinion gear shaft. If the effective, mean contact radius for the ring gear is 116 mm and the corresponding contact radius for the input pinion is 22.5 mm, the effective gear ratio driving the system is 5.15, and the motion driving the system is given as:

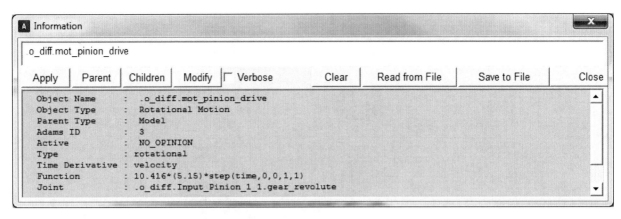

Figure 119 Motion Applied to Input Pinion

It should be noted that the UDE permits the motion to be specified on the input gear revolute and that the step function with time is employed in order to smoothly ramp on the motion, thereby avoiding possible problems associated with unrealistic and undesired start-up transients.

Mechanism Constraints – Applied Loading

In the "Determination of Wheel Loading" section above, it was computed that the right wheel (and, hence, right axle shaft) must turn 1.577 times faster than the left wheel because it is traveling a greater distance in the turn. This is, in effect, a constraint on the gear train acting between the two axle shafts but imposed by tire contact with ground. However, the tire/ground contact is not explicitly defined in the model, since there are no tires, and it must be imposed on the system. If the left shaft is constrained to turn at the inside tire velocity while the ring gear is driven at the mean spin velocity specified above, the outer shaft will, in theory, be compelled to spin at the angular velocity of the outside wheel. We shall see.

Because the shaft constraints are generated by UDEs, the markers specifying the joints are no longer easily accessible for further additions or modifications, and, as was the case with the ring gear shaft housings, additional parts which *can* be accessed must be added and locked to any gear part shaft being constrained. Since the shaft/ground constraint only touches the left (inside) shaft, only one dummy part is needed. However, should additional system modifications be desired, possibly effecting both shafts, a dummy part will also be added to the right shaft for the sake of generality. These additional parts will be massless. The figure below shows the left and right shaft dummy parts (the magenta disks), which are each locked to their respective shafts at any convenient point along their shaft axes.

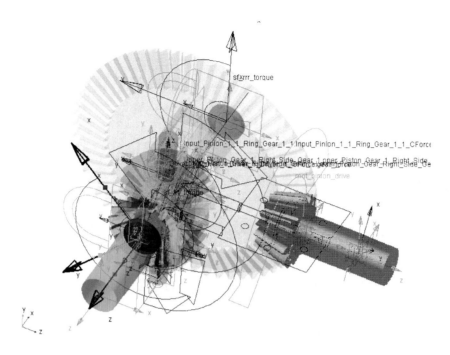

Figure 120 Axle Shaft Dummy Parts

In the figure, the part transparencies have been adjusted for convenience by selecting the parts and using the sliding scale "Appearance" button to adjust the part specularity.

The imposed motion (using an Adams "GCON") cited above must apply the proper constraint relation between the black triad and ground on the left shaft in the figure above. Because the disks are uniform and orthogonal, the dummy part CG markers are aligned precisely with their shaft spin axes and can be used. It should be noted that, although the disks are massless, the user can still specify zeroed mass and inertia properties for the parts, as long as they are locked in all 6 directions to a part which *does* provide the requisite mass properties.

The GCON definition is shown below.

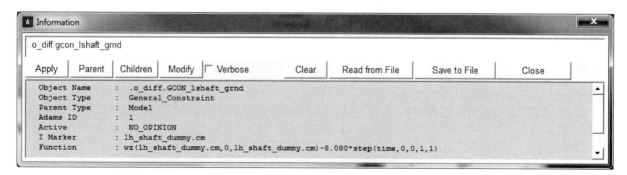

Figure 121 Left/Right Shaft GCON Constraint Definition

When a GCON function is evaluated during an Adams solution, the defining function expression is *always* driven to zero. The defining kinematic freedoms take the form **wz(i,j,k)** →where **i** identifies the constrained marker; **j** identifies the reference triad relative to which the motion takes (a 0 selects the ground origin by default); and **k** is the reference triad which defines the spin direction. In words, the

function above reads: "in global coordinates, step the left hand shaft up to its full speed about its Z-axis over the same interval as the input pinion is brought up to its full speed."

It should be noted that the addition of the two dummy parts adds 12 DOFs to the system, the 2 fixed joints locking the dummy parts to the shafts removes the 12 DOFs just added, and that the GCON removes yet another DOF.

Mechanism Restraints – Applied Loading

In addition to the constraint coupling the spin velocities of the 2 shafts, the torques due to tire rolling resistance must be added to their respective shafts. These are applied as constant-value, action-only torques applied to the dummy part CG markers. The torque applied to the left shaft is given below.

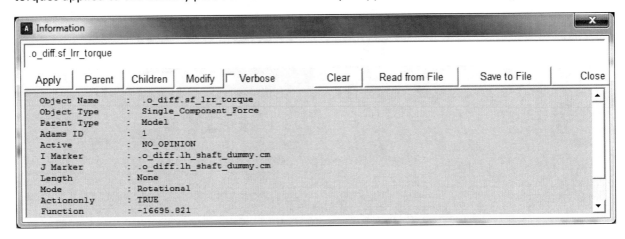

Figure 122 Applied Rolling Resistance Torque -- Left Shaft

The right shaft torque has the same form but references the right dummy part CMG marker.

Differential Model Gruebler Count

In all of the preceding modeling, great care has been taken to track the system Gruebler count, and this practice will be maintained for this model.

The total DOF count introduced by the parts is:

72)

$$DOF = (11 - 1) * 6 = +60$$

The DOFs removed by the constraints are:

73)

$$DOF_{revolutes} = 6 * -5 = -30$$

$$DOF_{fixed} = 4 * -6) = -24$$

$$DOF_{motions} = 1 * -1 = -1$$

$$DOF_{gcons} = 1 * -1 = -1$$

The resulting freedom count is +60 − 56 =+4. In effect, there is one dynamic DOF for each of the 5 gear sets, less 1 DOF for the GCON constraint connecting the left and right shafts.

This can be checked by executing a **Tools/Model Verify** command string within Adams/View for the differential model which yields:

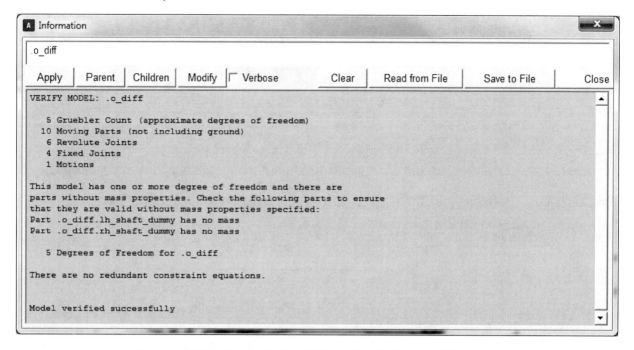

Figure 123 Model Verify for Differential Model Gruebler Count

Alas, an inconsistency appears to have arisen, and the verify command claims a DOF count of 5! What could be the cause of this? The answer lies in the nature of the specified constraint. In the classical sense, constraints are fundamentally ***displacement***-based. In Adams, a velocity- or acceleration-based constraint does not functionally exist until time begins to "flow" in the simulation. A Model Verify command is performed at time t=0, thus these constraints do not yet exist numerically. This fact was overlooked in the manual DOF determination associated with equations 72 and 73. The lesson is this: the Gruebler expression can generate confusion for the user in certain situations. Nonetheless, it is still good practice to perform a Gruebler count on any model under consideration.

Differential Model Results

The model is executed for 2 simulation seconds at a time step resolution of 0.01 seconds. The figure below gives the pinion input velocity together with the resulting left and right shaft speeds.

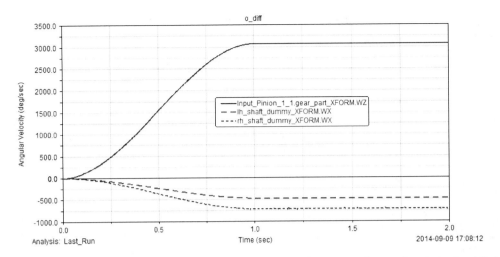

Figure 124 Input Pinion(red) Left Shaft (blue) Right Shaft(magenta) Angular Velocity Histories

The plot below gives the actions of the rolling resistance torques on the dummy shaft parts.

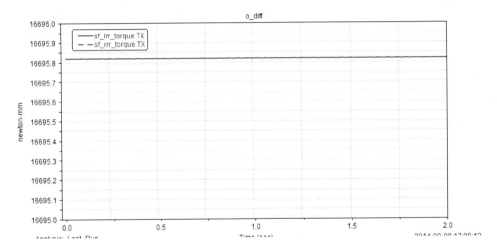

Figure 125 Applied Rolling Resistance Torques

The model contact force history is saved in a CONTACT_INCIDENTS list, which is accessed using the model browser sequence: **All Other/Contact Incident Containers/Contact_Incidents/info**. A typical output, which gives the time at which the system 3D CONTACT forces reached convergence, is shown below.

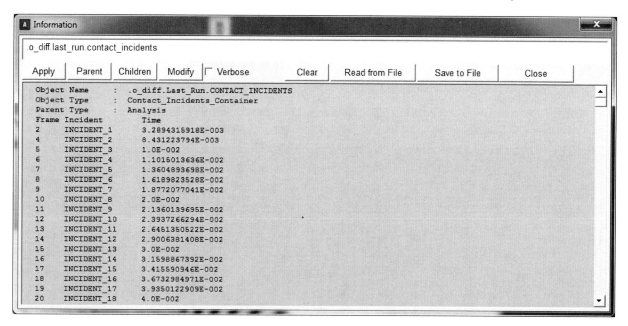

Figure 126 CONTACT_INCIDENTS List

Using, again, the model browser, the statistics for each incident are available as well using **All Other/ Incident /INCIDENT_#/info**.

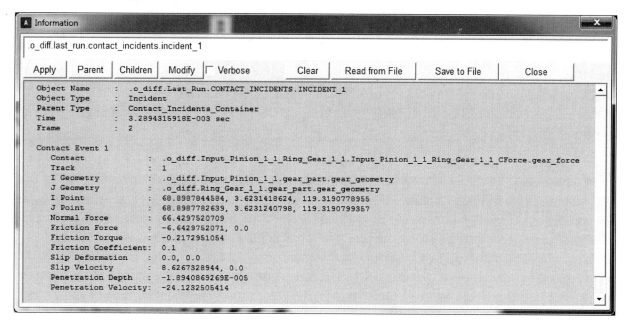

Figure 127 Contact Data for INCIDENT_1

The figure above merits some comment.

1) The I-J Geometry labels identify the gear parts in contact.
2) The I-J Point labels locate the end points of the contact normal vector defined by the volumetric intersection of the two gear parts.
3) The Normal Force is the action/reaction force acting along the normal vector on the gear pair.

4) The Friction Force & Friction Torque are computed from the projection of the relative part slip velocities onto a plane defined using the intersection volume.

5) The Penetration Depth and Penetration Velocity are used with the contact stiffness and damping coefficients to determine the contact forces.

The sought-after drive torque exerted by the pinion gear is shown below.

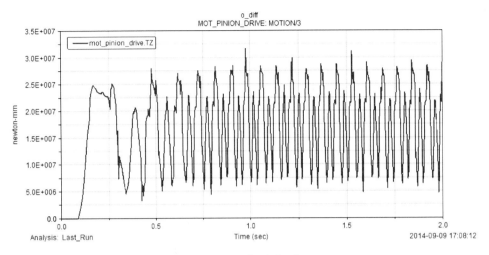

Figure 128 Pinion (Driving) Torque

Differential Model Results – Comments

From figure 124 it can be seen that, after the system is brought up to speed, the pinion velocity is 3073 deg/sec, the left shaft velocity is 462.9 deg/sec, and the right shaft velocity is 730 deg/sec. This is precisely the speed ratio of 1.577 which was sought, and it demonstrates that the kinematic behavior of the differential model is correct.

Figure 128 provides the initial answer sought by the problem. The drive torque is highly oscillatory, bouncing between 5.0e6 and 3.7e7 N-mm. That the results are so variable should not be surprising. The gear stiffnesses are high, the applied wheel torques due to rolling resistance (only) are modest, but the left and right shaft inertias, since they do not include any of the masses that would be connected outboard (the wheels, CV joints, associated shafting, etc.), are low. Nor do they include any mass damping which might be associated with the translational inertia of the vehicle mass. This effect might be approximated for each shaft by taking half the vehicle mass multiplied by the square of the wheel rolling radius and applying it as an instantaneous "pseudo inertia" (667 kg * 400 mm^2 = 1.0672E+09 kg-mm^2) to the dummy part locked to each shaft. Presuming they can be defended as reasonably realistic, these applied loading changes would increase the structural loading on the differential appreciably. Figure 129 below plots the drive torque with these elevated inertias added.

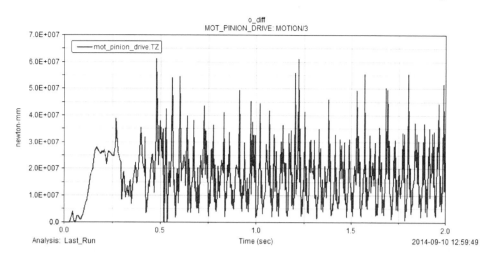

Figure 129 Drive Torque with 'Pseudo Inertias' Acting on the Shafts

The additional inertial loading on the shafts has roughly doubled the gear loads and sharpened the gear contact "spikes."

Some questions for the reader:

1) Presuming it could be done, how would the inclusion of, say, shaft flexibility change the latest answers?

2) Without modeling the gear meshing as flex-on-flex contact (technically feasible, but costly in terms of compute times), how could the left/right (axle) shafts be modified to approximate the flexibility associated with tire carcass deflection and shaft wind-up? (Hint: replace the shaft dummy part fixed joints with revolute joints and employ torsional spring-dampers to restrain the released, torsional freedoms.

Some Further Notes on ADAMS Solvers

If there is any aspect of ADAMS MBD analysis that bears with it the aroma of "magic," it is the numerical solvers used to deliver the problem answers. They can be marvelous in their sophistication and intimidating in their complexity. Their importance cannot be over-stated.

The descriptions that follow will probably lack the sophistication that the topic deserves, but will, hopefully, provide a useful, if cursory, look into the similarities and differences of the available solver options.

Solver Options

As of this writing, there are 8 different solvers available to the user. However, the ADAMS user need not feel faint when confronted by such a panoply of choices. For most models, the number actually used in practice is relatively limited.

Note: As of this writing, two versions of the solver code are available to the user: **F77(FORTRAN)** and **CXX(C++)**. F77 is legacy code, and has been in a state of stasis for some years. It lacks many of the latest code enhancements available through C++ and will, in all probability, eventually disappear from the ADAMS code. All of the modeling in this book employs the C++ solver.

GSTIFF

The venerable GSTIFF integrator is the original solver used when ADAMS was first developed. It is based on theoretical work in numerical analysis published by Charles W. Gear at the University of Illinois. It is still widely used and, as of this date, remains the default solver for ADAMS. It is an implicit, predictor-corrector solver which functions essentially as described in the Theory section detailed above. It uses an (up to) 6th order predicting polynomial for all the problem state variables. The corrector phase, however, does *not* include the velocities and accelerations of the state variables, which are back-computed from division by the time step and the square of the time step, respectively. This explains why solutions fail (usually in an acceleration term) in a poorly-posed problem when the time step gets very small. Division by the square of a very small number approaches a divide by zero numerical condition, and the computer runs out of significant figures to cope with it.

The predicting polynomials are all defined by past points separated by a constant time step set at the beginning of the new time step. The interval used to define the separation of the predicting points is assumed to be a constant. If the predicting polynomial order is greater than 2, this can lead to numerical anomalies. For example, a joint displacement in a given constrained direction may be (correctly) computed to be zero, but the corresponding acceleration and velocity are non-zero, as are any associated forces(!). And, when plotted, they appear as very short-duration "spikes." Since the velocity and acceleration are successive time derivatives of the (zero!) displacement, this cannot be correct. These anomalous spikes usually appear only if the solver Index (see below) is at **I3**, the order of this predicting polynomial is high and the time step is changing. Changes to the Index can alleviate this problem.

WSTIFF

The Wielenga stiff integrator, in order to avoid the "spikes" sometimes seen when the GSTIFF solver is used, replaces the algorithm used in GSTIFF (determined from the so-called Nordsieck array) to generate predicting polynomials using an interpolation algorithm which correctly accounts for changes in previous, converged time step intervals. This change can lead to appreciably increased solution times when WSTIFF is employed.

CONSTANT_BDF

(Not supported in the C++ solver.)

ABAM

The Adams-Bashforth Adams-Moulton integrator removes the constraint variables from the solution set, and then solves the reduced equation set explicitly. The solution is single-step. It is only practical if the system being analyzed contains high-frequency content for the full solution duration. It is almost never used in ADAMS. (Not supported in the C++ solver.)

RKF45

The Runge-Kutta-Fehlberg (4.5) is an explicit, one-step solver. It is almost never used in ADAMS. (Not supported in the C++ solver.)

HHT

The Hilber-Hughes-Taylor integrator is an implicit solver. The predicting polynomial is limited to order 2. It is finding increased usage in ADAMS problems, although it tends to over-damp the solution results. The system Jacobian is updated at every solution step. This integrator is available only on C++.

Newmark

The Newmark integrator is an implicit solver. The predictor is limited to order 1. The system Jacobian is updated at every solution step. This integrator is available only on C++. It, likewise, is seldom used in ADAMS.

HASTIFF

The Hiller Anantharaman stiff integrator, like the WSTIFF integrator, takes variations in the step sizes used to generate the predicting polynomial into account. This integrator is available only on C++.

Index Options

The index of a solver is determined by the order of differentiation of the problem constraint equations. In general, the higher the index order, the more discontinuous the constraints tend to become, as typified by the potential for anomalous "spikes" described under GSTIFF above.

Index 3 (I3)

I3 solutions generally differentiate the constraint functions 3 times. This is the default index for integrators GSTIFF/WSTIFF/HHT.

Stabilized Index 2 (SI2)

SI2 solutions reduce the constraint differentiation to order 2 by including the system velocities in the corrector computations. Solver stability and robustness are improved since accelerations are determined by dividing velocity terms by the time step and not the time step squared. The SI2 formulation is available for GSTIFF, WSTIFF, CONSTANT_BDF, and HASTIFF integrators only. A disadvantage is that the solution time will increase, sometimes appreciably.

Special note: Nicki Orlandea, the "daddy" of ADAMS and one of the true Titans of MBD, has stated firmly that, in his opinion, GSTIFF SI2 should be the solver of choice.

Stabilized Index 1 (SI1)

SI1 solutions reduce the constraint differentiation to order 1 by including the system accelerations and velocities in the corrector computations. Solver stability and robustness are further improved. For the F77 code, the SI1 formulation is available for the GSTIFF, WSTIFF, and CONSTANT_BDF solvers. For the C++ code, SI1 formulation is available for HASTIFF integrator only. A disadvantage associated with SI1 is that the solution time can increase *very* appreciably.

Corrector Options

As detailed in the theory section above, once the predictor has estimated the changes to all the variables, the corrector must determine changes in the variables necessary to solve the equations stably and accurately. Depending on which solver is being employed, the user can "adjust" the corrector activity appreciably. Note that this should be done *only if the user knows what he/she is doing*! Otherwise, the user should rely on the default settings for the solver in question, which are based on

copious field experience. For starters, and to gain a feel for what is possible, the user might consider *modest* changes to the **INTEGRATOR/** settings detailed below.

Error

Determines the permissible solution convergence error. Loosening the error tolerance tends to make solution convergence easier, while simultaneously making the answers less rigorous. As was mentioned above, when employing implicit solvers, the answers are truly accurate only when successive tightening of the requested error results in little or no change in analysis results.

HINIT

Defines the initial time step. Its value defaults to 1/20th of the requested output step. It can be tightened to help an analysis start if it is experiencing difficulties.

HMAX

Defines the maximum time step permitted. If HMAX is less than the requested output step, the effective error tolerance is also tightened. (See INTERPOLATE below.)

HMIN

Defines the minimum time step permitted.

Note: 0 < or = HMIN < or = HINIT < or = HMAX

INTERPOLATE

INTERPOLATE = ON releases the integrator from the requirement that its step size be regulated to force system convergence at all requested output steps. Any over-stepped output points have their system values calculated by interpolation back to them and the interpolated values are then refined ("reconciled") to satisfy the equilibrium and constraint equations. (Defaults: OFF → GSTIFF, WSTIFF; ON → ABAM; Not supported → CONSTANT_BDF, RFK45.)

Special Note: If HMAX is set sufficiently small, and INTERPOLATE is OFF, the ERROR setting may be, in effect, *ignored*, and reducing it to confirm the solution accuracy will automatically yield the same solution, thereby giving a false indication of a converged (and accurate) numerical solution!

KMAX

The maximum order used in the solution polynomials. Should be employed only by experienced users.

PATTERN

Indicates the pattern to be used for the Jacobian (corrector) evaluations. TRUE or FALSE character strings are concatenated to define this. Default: T:F:F:F:T:F:F:F:T:F (for GSTIFF and WSTIFF); Default F (for HHT and Newmark). This should be employed only by experienced users.

CORRECTOR = original

Requires that, at convergence, the error in all solution variables be less than the corrector error tolerance. This is the default.

CORRECTOR = modified

Requires that, at convergence, the error for only integrated variables be less than the corrector error tolerance. This is a less stringent corrector criterion and should be used with circumspection.

For further possibilities, the reader is directed to the substantial on-line help available in VIEW by clicking on the question mark in the blue circle and then performing a "search" of ADAMS/Help on the key word "Integrator."

The ADAMS 3D Pendulum ... Revisited

At the risk of being pedantic, let us re-visit the pendulum model for the purpose of emphasizing, yet again, the importance of attention to error control. The initial pendulum model (refer to figure 11) was executed using the GSTIFF SI2 integrator (Nicki Orlandea's integrator of choice) with a very tight error control of 1.0e-5. The best way to gain a conceptual "feel" for what this means is to think of the model length units, although the error criterion is purely numerical and will be applied to all state variables, regardless of their nature. In effect, the error for the pendulum is being set to 1.0e-5 meters. For the pendulum results shown below, the GSTIFF INDEX has been re-set from SI2 to I3, and the model has been executed with 3 increasingly relaxed ERROR settings. The figure below compares the pendulum's angular displacement (the pendulum arm's LPRF Euler PSI displacement) for the 3 runs.

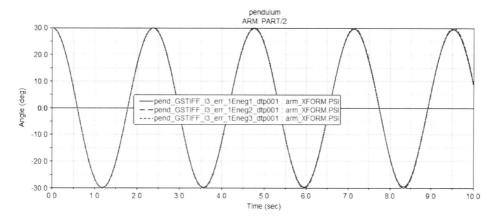

Figure 130 Pendulum Arm Angular Displacement: ERROR=1e-3 --> 1e-2 --> 1e-1

The reader will notice that, at the end of the 4th cycle, the curves seem to be separating. The figure below concentrates on this part of the plot for the last second of the simulation.

123

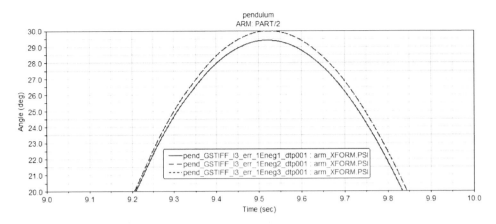

Figure 131 ADAMS 3D Pendulum -- Motion Degradation Due to Lax ERROR Setting

Clearly, the loosening of the error tolerance from 1.0e-2 to 1.0e-1 has resulted in the system beginning to (incorrectly) "leak" energy! The peak angular displacement has dropped from the expected 30 degrees to ~29.4 degrees after 4 swing cycles. Further indication of the bad things that can happen if the error tolerance is too sloppy is shown below.

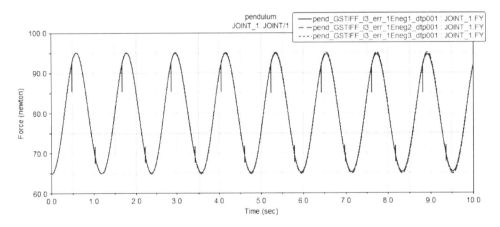

Figure 132 Constraint 'Spike' Anomalies due to Lax ERROR setting

The lesson, hopefully, is clear…

Some Historical Successes

The author is very proud that MSC's products have played, and continue to play, a significant role in the success of many of the world's most prestigious engineering organizations. Some of these successes are mundane but nonetheless important to those organizations achieving them. Others involve drama on a nearly cosmic scale. A case in point is NASA's Curiosity Martian lander and its now famous "7 minutes of terror" related to the spacecraft's orbital descent to a "soft" landing. While NASA has a long history of using Adams to evaluate a host of landing systems, the Curiosity lander represented perhaps the most challenging evaluation to date. The functioning of the Curiosity system is extremely complex, as can be seen from the figure below.

Figure 133 Computer Animation of Curiosity Being Lowered to the Martian Surface (NASA)

It is difficult to contemplate even fabricating such complex systems without first challenging their design concepts analytically with high-fidelity "virtual prototypes" generated by Adams and, thus, gaining a measure of confidence in their functionality. It is important to note that NASA did all of this event modeling themselves. It is most gratifying to see users challenge the Adams software capabilities and succeed so spectacularly.

While it is the author's contention that no mechanical system should ever be rendered in hardware without first completing sufficient engineering analysis to generate a reasonable level of confidence that the hardware will work, there are times when a forensic Adams model of an already-existing system needs to be created. Such is the case with vehicular accident reconstruction. A case in point is the crash

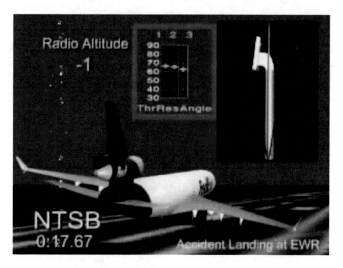

Figure 134 Aircraft at Critical, 2nd Right Main Gear Contact (NTSB)

of an MD-11, wide-body cargo transport aircraft while landing at Newark airport in 1997. The National Transportation Safety Board (NTSB) completed an extremely comprehensive survey of the crash site and, at the very start of the debris field, found a suspicious piece of wreckage: a failed, high tensile-strength bolt from an inboard support fitting on the aircraft right main landing gear. A review of the landing gear structural design analysis by the airframe manufacturer failed to provide any insight into a possible cause of the bolt failure. To examine a potential failure hypothesis, an Adams model featuring a

simplified, rigid airframe model with a flexible right main landing gear modeled in some detail using Adams structural elements was "flown" on a controlled landing descent using the aircraft DFDR (Digital Flight Data Recorder) "black box" history up to the point when the recorders dropped "off line" as the aircraft began to break up (reference [7]). When the initial Adams results confirmed the suspect bolt loads were not sufficient to result in failure, the model fidelity came into question, and the simplified airframe was replaced by a more comprehensive, flexible airframe generated using the MSC Nastran FEA code. However, this, too, failed to predict the bolt failure. The flexible airframe model was further modified to permit non-linear, Adams-generated boundary conditions to be applied to the linear MSC Nastran airframe model to simulate a primary structural failure. When this was done, the tire traces from the Adams model closely matched an apparent spacing anomaly in the tire skid marks cited in the NTSB crash survey, and the mystery was solved. Pilot control inputs had resulted in an overload condition on the right main gear which had caused the aircraft rear wing spar web to fail, and the subsequent, excessive wing deflection had pried the suspect bolt loose as the aircraft began to break up. The bolt was not the cause of the failure but a consequence of it. The Adams analysis was cited in the NTSB final report.

The ability to rapidly model and analytically evaluate complex systems can be good for an organization's "bottom line." An organization originally created to provide consulting support to the automotive racing industry developed the capability to rapidly generate full vehicle models using Adams. When an opportunity arose to expand their consulting activities into the defense industry, this skill paid dividends. The opportunity in question did not permit their customer the luxury of employing the build/test/re-build/re-test development methodology on the vehicle in question. There simply wasn't time. To capture the business, they had to be sure the first rendition of the vehicle in hardware was "right."

Figure 135 Military Rough Terrain Vehicle Model (Pratt & Miller)

The effort went from a "clean sheet of paper" to a test-worthy vehicle in the stunningly short time of 12 weeks, and the hardware performed as predicted by the Adams analysis.

The design of deployable arrays to provide power to orbiting satellites constitutes a very challenging design problem. The cost/mass ratio of putting an object in orbit is extremely high, and the urgency

involved in lowering this value never ceases. The issue is further complicated by the need to package a potentially enormous deployable structure in the smallest stowed volume possible. This almost invariably results in the use of the smallest forces possible to affect the deployment. Any attempt to test such a deployment design in the test lab is always going to be confronted by a Newtonian demon...... *gravity!* Attempts to minimize this effect in laboratory testing, such as positioning the satellite such that gravity is perpendicular to the primary deployment direction and employing additional, fictitious, moving supports in (hopefully) friction-less tracks is often unsatisfyingly approximate, or simply wrong, introducing as they do a host of effects which will not be experienced when deployment of the hardware is initiated in orbit. A high-fidelity Adams model obviates the necessity of such extreme and questionable trickery. A case in point is shown below.

Figure 136 Curwin Solar Panel Array Model -- Deployed (Fokker Space)

The Adams model revealed the dangers of allowing a passive, uncontrolled array deployment and led to the use of a staged, controlled deployment design.

The importance of a holistic, that is, complete, system model cannot be over-estimated. Even if a (sub-) system design has been proven viable in one field application, changes to another component in the system with which it directly, or even indirectly interacts, can result in undesirable behavior. A manufacturer of powertrain components must match its transmission products with "upstream" components (engines) and "downstream" components (drive axles). The figure below shows an Adams model of a heavy vehicle transmission comprised of 14 gears. The interaction of the driveline components is central to the NVH behavior of the full system.

Figure 137 Transmission Model (Scania)

The Adams model had to possess the correct torsional stiffness properties if it were to exhibit the correct behavior. After building a model of a system for which results were already available and comparing the test data with the Adams results (the critical system frequencies were in very good agreement), the powertrain manufacturer could confidently evaluate different system configurations for which test data didn't exist and have confidence that the Adams virtual prototype possessed a high measure of fidelity. The claim was made that quality issues were resolved "30 percent to 40 percent faster" when running simulations and test measurements because the Adams model allowed the product to be better understood.

The cases cited above, while representing only a smattering of significant applications of Adams to generate realistic "virtual prototypes" of complex systems since its inception, will, hopefully, provide a prospective user some idea as to what is possible using the Adams software.

Concluding Comments

As this is written, the author has been privileged to work with Adams and its related software products continuously for over 33 years. It all started when he was astonished in 1981 to see an animation of a very simple, 3-piece, compound pendulum cavorting in what was clearly a *very* non-linear fashion. Exposed as an undergraduate engineering student to the basics of Lagrangian dynamics, he knew just enough to be stunned by what he was seeing and to appreciate it. Having just lost a colleague, killed while performance testing a competitor's materials handling vehicle, he decided to see if such a vehicle's behavior could be analytically predicted with any success by Adams. It could (reference [6]), and two years later he joined MDI to enjoy working with Adams full-time. The vast expansion of the Adams code capabilities, especially with regard to the growing intimacy with Finite Element methods, which have ensued since the acquisition of MDI by MSC Software are nothing short of breath-taking. Over that extensive time span, it has *never* gotten boring! The author sincerely wishes the reader of this modest book a similar experience.

Appendix I – Principal Adams Modeling Elements

The modeling elements described below represent those most commonly used to construct MBD models within Adams. For those elements not described below, the reader is referred to the Adams on-line documentation which can be accessed directly within the Adams software.

As noted earlier in the book, capital letters (e.g., "PART") are generally used to denote keywords and parameters in the Adams or MSC Nastran modeling languages; however, in practice capitalization is not necessary for the these keywords and parameters.

Body Types

There are several different types of bodies which can be employed in Adams. The selection will depend on the nature of the component in question and also on the purpose of the analysis. Descriptions of the body types are given in what follows.

PART

By far, the most ubiquitous element used to represent a discrete component in Adams is the PART. The reader has already been surreptitiously introduced to the PART in the preceding theoretical analysis of the simple pendulum. In general:

1) By default, when models are built using Adams-based coding, PART/1 of any model defaults to the GROUND PART. GROUND is the Newtonian inertial reference frame. Its origin is the "Center of the Universe" for an Adams model.

2) Every (non-GROUND) PART contains a unique origin, known as the Local Part Reference Frame (LPRF) which is used as the reference coordinate system for any point of interest on the PART (refer to figure 5). If the LPRF location and orientation are not explicitly specified, its starting position defaults to the global origin. Besides positioning the PART in the model assembly, the Adams PART statement is also used to specify any initial velocity conditions desired as well as to control the PART positioning during the analysis initial conditions phase.

3) A PART can as extensive as desired. It can have a full set of mass properties, as does our pendulum example (refer to figure 11), or it can be devoid of extent and consist of a single MARKER triad only. Massless PARTs, as long as they are completely constrained, are also feasible.

4) The geometric representation of a PART can be extensive if it is, say, represented by a Parasolid file, or it can be a simple stick figure represented by Adams OUTLINE statements connecting user-specified MARKERs.

5) Each PART employed will add 15 equations (6 position, 6 velocity, and 3 angular momentum) to the model equation count.

6) When building Adams models from PART geometry generated by graphical pre-processors, collections of PARTs which move as a whole should be modeled as a single PART. If each geometric entity in a non-articulating assembly were rendered as an individual Part and all the PARTs were then locked together using FIXED constraints, the model equation set size could quickly become intractable.

POINT MASS

If an MBD model component's extent and/or orientation are unimportant, a POINT_MASS may be employed. All rotational effects drop away and only 6 equations (3 translational positions and 3 translational velocities) are needed. The POINT_MASS has proven useful in the analysis of deploying net or cable arrays where the cord or cable bending/torsion effects can be neglected. GROUND cannot be defined as a POINT_MASS.

FLEXBODY

Component flexibility can be extremely significant in obtaining the correct results for many system models. The maximum structural forces experienced by an aircraft model performing a landing can easily differ by as much as 50% between rigid and flexible representations of the same flight vehicle. The path followed by a ground vehicle at speed will usually differ appreciably if its suspension and chassis are rendered flexible. Prediction of satellite behavior is highly dependent on the correct incorporation of flexible effects. Few things are more poignant than the telemetry traces of a satellite in orbit destroying itself because its attitude control system was designed without correctly including structural flexibility effects.

Adams addresses this need by permitting the user to create linearly elastic FLEXBODYs from Finite Element Analysis (FEA) models. While the details of the FEA steps required to form the FLEXBODY are beyond the scope of this book, the fundamental features needed for the element will be described. It should be mentioned that MSC Software, Inc., the developers of the MSC/Adams product, also produce the MSC/MSC Nastran finite element code, and the synergy between these two products has become increasingly intimate.

Fundamentally, the FLEXBODY is a reduced DOF, modal condensation of an FEA model defined in Cartesian space. As such, it reduces the usually very large elastic DOF count of the defining model to a greatly reduced DOF count expressed in modal coordinates. The excavator boom example from text example 2 is a good indicator of the possible DOF reduction, while still maintaining the correct structural behavior. The modal FLEXBODY is contained in a Modal Neutral File (MNF). In a well-conditioned structure, the frequency and mode shape correlation with an FEA modal analysis of the full structure will correlate within a few percent.

General Requirements
1) The FEA structure must be a single, contiguous, linearly-elastic body. It must not possess mechanism freedoms.
2) The FEA modal reduction should always be performed on a free-free structure.
3) Because modal condensation tends to degrade the accuracy of the higher modes in the spectrum, the number of modes retained should be such that the highest modal frequency of interest should be at the midpoint of the retained MNF spectrum.
4) At those connection points and connection directions where correct flexibility is important, the associated nodes/GRIDs should be modeled as "master" points to capture exact properties at those points. In a MSC Nastran SOL103 modal condensation analysis, these GRIDs will be specified in the ASET declaration.

5) While it is possible to selectively delete MNF modes, this should generally not be done, since it may remove critical DOF content from the FLEXBODY. Instead, undesired modes should be dynamically suppressed by the application of critical damping.

6) The linear behavior of the FLEXBODY can be corrupted in an Adams solution by excessive structural deflection (i.e., beyond the linear limit) or by high spin velocities. Such velocities require non-linear elastic coupling terms which are not present in the linear MNF structure.

Restraints (Force-Based Modeling Entities)

Adams offers an extensive selection of restraint (i.e., differential-based) elements. In general, these elements will be defined by an I MARKER upon which the defined forces act, a J MARKER to which the reactions are applied, and a reference RM MARKER which supplies the force component orientations, should they differ from global or be otherwise undefined. The algorithms defining the force components will, depending on the type of force, be specified using just constants, or expressions comprised of algorithms defined from the extensive Adams function library, or even expressions provided by user-supplied subroutines.

GFORCE

The general force – GFORCE – applies (up to) 6 user-defined force components (3 translational forces and 3 torques) on the I MARKER.

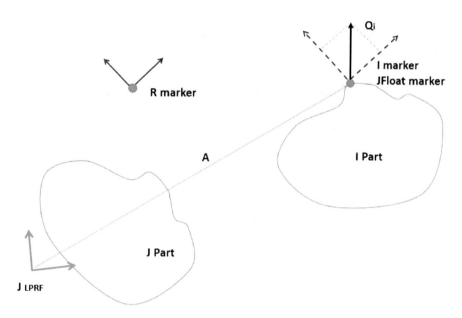

Figure a1 GFORCE Schematic

The J MARKER is of the "floating" variety and is entered as a JFLOAT entity. Unlike a standard MARKER which is fixed in both position and orientation to the PART on which it is defined, the JFLOAT MARKER moves coincidentally in space with the GFORCE I MARKER and defines an instantaneous moment arm (vector A) back to the J PART local part reference frame (LPRF).

A1)

$$\{Q_I^R\} = \begin{Bmatrix} F_I \\ T_I \end{Bmatrix} = \left[g(Y, \dot{Y}, t) \right]$$

Where g is virtually any desired function of the system state variables Y. Superscript R represents the coordinate system in which the force components act, and F and T identify the 6 Q's as Cartesian forces and torques.

The instantaneous reactions on the J MARKER PART are determined from this moment arm and the I MARKER applied force actions in the RM orientation.

A2)

$$\vec{F}_J = -\vec{F}_I$$

$$\vec{T}_J = -\vec{T}_I - \vec{A} \times \vec{F}_I$$

Note that the I and J MARKERS **must** be on different model PARTs. Each model GFORCE adds 6 equations to an Adams equation set.

It should be noted that

1) The GFORCE can be virtually any function which acts between 2 PARTs.
2) The defining equations can be coupled or uncoupled.
3) Discontinuous functions can be employed, but to do so, except in very special circumstances, will almost invariably lead to analysis failure.
4) The generalized coordinates for this element are Cartesian orthogonal.

VFORCE
The vector force – VFORCE – is merely a GFORCE minus any rotational force components. Thus, it adds only 3 equations to a system.

VTORQUE
The vector torque – VTORQUE – is merely a GFORCE minus any translational force components. Thus, it, too, adds only 3 equations to a system.

SFORCE
The single component force – SFORCE – applies a single vector component force or torque to a MARKER set. Depending on its definition, this component may be a translational force or a rotational torque. Further, it may or may not have a defined reaction. It is a very powerful algorithm, possessing some unusual features, so it will be described in some detail.

The general form of the SFORCE is

A3)

$$\{Q_I^J\} = \{F_I\} = \left[g(Y, \dot{Y}, t) \right]$$

Where, like the GFORCE, g can be almost any function definable in terms of the state variables. The forces above are *actions* on the I-MARKER.

ACTION/REACTION SFORCE – TRANSLATION

The direction of an action/reaction SFORCE is determined by the instantaneous displacement vector running from the J MARKER to the I MARKER. Consider it a "spanning" vector. The instantaneous SFORCE velocity is obtained from the summation of the projections of the MARKER global velocities onto the spanning vector. The key to the resultant force sense is that "positive forces repel" the I-J MARKER pair. The figure below illustrates this.

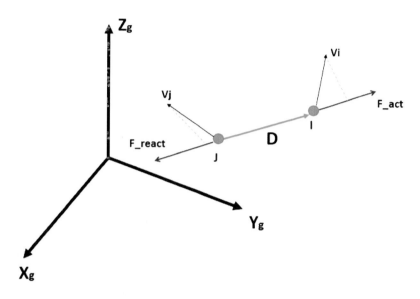

Figure a2 Action/Reaction SFORCE Direction Definition

In the figure, a net, positive resultant force due to the instantaneous displacement and velocity states of the IJ MARKER set has been assumed.

It is obvious from the figure that, If the I and J MARKERs should ever coincide, the SFORCE becomes undefined. If this happens and the Adams analyst is lucky, this will cause a fatal run-time error. If the Adams analyst is *unlucky*, and the integrator step-sizing is sufficiently coarse, the SFORCE may go "over-center" with the force ends "swapping place," leading to incorrect results.

The *reactions* on the J-MARKER are

A4)

$$\vec{F}_J = -\vec{F}_I$$

A translational, action/reaction SFORCE adds 5 equations to an Adams model: length, force magnitude, and force x-, y-, and z-components.

ACTION/REACTION SFORCE – ROTATION

An action/reaction rotational SFORCE applies the action torque to the I-MARKER about its Z-axis, and the reaction torque to the J-MARKER, also about its Z-axis. The I- and J-MARKERs *must* be defined such that

their Z-axes remain parallel, although they need not be co-directed. If this condition is not maintained, errors will result. The force relationship is sketched below.

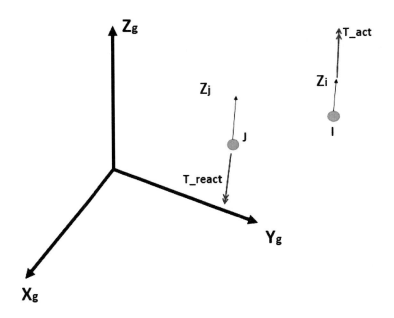

Figure a3 Action/Reaction Torsional SFORCE

It should be noted that the I & J-MARKERS need not be coincident, but they will be so in the vast majority of applications. The 3D pendulum model with the added hinge restraint from the Theory section employs an action/reaction torsional SFORCE applied to an IJ MARKER pair in which the MARKERs are coincident with their Z-axes parallel and co-directed.

The **reactions** on the J-MARKER are

A5)

$$\vec{T}_J = -\vec{T}_I$$

An action/reaction rotational SFORCE adds 1 equation to the system.

ACTION-ONLY SFORCE – TRANSLATION
An action-only translational SFORCE applies the defined force in the I-MARKER in the instantaneous direction of the J-MARKER Z-axis.

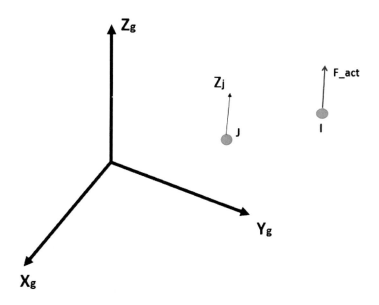

Figure a4 Translational Action-Only SFORCE

Note that, for the action-only translational force, it is possible to specify the *identical* MARKER ID for both the I- and J-MARKERs. This is the only instance in the Adams code where this is allowed. A practical example of this type of application is, say, a rocket nozzle. The rocket exhaust does not, in general, *push* on anything. Rather it provides thrust by generating a change in the propellant mass momentum.

A translational, action-only SFORCE likewise adds 5 equations to an Adams model, but the expressions are devoid of reactions.

ACTION-ONLY SFORCE – ROTATION
The rotational action-only SFORCE is analogous to its translational counterpart except a torque is applied.

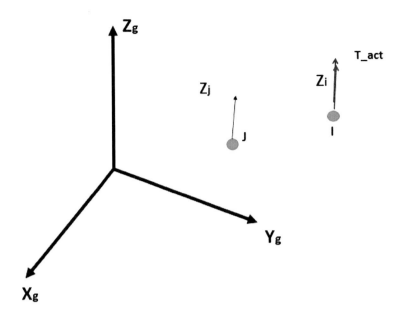

Figure a5 Torsional Action-Only SFORCE

A use for this might be found in the modeling of the ancient Greek Aeolipile.

Figure a6 The First Turbine -- An Ancient Greek Aeolipile [source -- Wikipedia]

Like the action/reaction rotational SFORCE, the action-only rotational SFORCE adds 1 equation to the system equation set which is devoid of any reaction terms.

BUSHING

The BUSHING element is a constitutively linear element capable of applying up to 6 force components

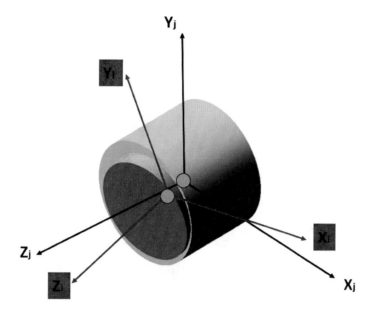

Figure a7 BUSHING Element (Loaded)

(3 translational and 3 rotational) on its defining MARKER set. A BUSHING adds 12 variables and equations to an Adams model. The first 6 are displacement values, and the last 6 are force values

A6)

$$\begin{Bmatrix} \Delta_i^J \\ Q_k^J \end{Bmatrix}; i = 1, \cdots 6; k = 7, \cdots 12$$

where

A7)

$$\{\Delta_i^J\} = \begin{Bmatrix} (\vec{\delta} \cdot \hat{\jmath}) \\ (\vec{\theta} \cdot \hat{\jmath}) \end{Bmatrix}$$

A8)

$$\{Q_k^J\} = -[K_{kk}]\{q_k\} - [C_{kk}]\{\dot{q}_k\} + \{Qo_k\}; k = 7, \cdots 12$$

Where q_i signifies the x-, y-, z-, rotation x-, rotation y-, and rotation z-directions as defined by the J-MARKER triad, K_{kk} is the (*diagonal* and constant) stiffness value, C_{kk} is the (*diagonal* and constant) damping value, and Qo_k is the (constant) pre-load in the q_k direction. Superscript J indicates the orientation of the J-MARKER is used in the definition. Note that the equation above defines the ***actions*** on the I-MARKER.

The generalized force vector Q_k is comprised of 3 Cartesian translational forces and 3 Cartesian rotational torques

A9)

$$\{Q_k\} = \begin{Bmatrix} F_l \\ T_r \end{Bmatrix}; l = 1 \cdots 3; r = 4 \cdots 6$$

The **reactions** on the J-MARKER are calculated from

A10)

$$\vec{F}_J = -\vec{F}_l$$

$$\vec{T}_J = -\vec{T}_r - \vec{\delta} \times \vec{F}_l$$

Where δ is the instantaneous deformation vector from the J-MARKER to the I-MARKER and the pre-load terms have been ignored.

It should be noted that

1) The BUSHING is a *linear* element in its constitutive values. However, the BUSHING deformations will generally be iterated/non-linear.
2) The displacement and velocity coefficient matrices are diagonal, therefore the forces and torques are uncoupled.
3) The generalized coordinates for this element are Cartesian orthogonal.
4) Displacements and velocities are always defined as I relative to J in J's coordinate system.
5) The force at the J-MARKER will be equal and opposite to the force on the I-MARKER, but this will generally not be true for the torques.
6) There are biased limits on the rotational displacements. At least two of the angular displacements must remain smaller than ~10 degrees. If the x-rotation exceeds 90 degrees, the correctness of the Y-torque becomes problematical. If the y-rotation exceeds 90 degrees, the correctness of the X-torque becomes problematical. Only the Z-rotation can displace more than 90 degrees without degrading the BUSHING force values. For this reason, a BUSHING should always be oriented such that maximum spin takes place about the Z-direction.

A BUSHING element adds 12 equations (6 displacements and 6 force components) to the Adams model.

SPRINGDAMPER
A springdamper is a linearly-elastic, constant-property force element providing a single, action/reaction translational force or rotational torque. It is similar in behavior to the action/reaction SFORCE described above.

BEAM
The BEAM element employs, essentially, the classical, Euler-Timoshenko beam formulation based on the "Engineer's Theory of Bending." A typical beam element is shown below.

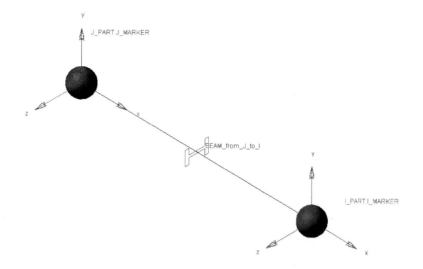

Figure a8 Adams BEAM Element

It should be emphasized that the BEAM element supplies forces *only*, with mass effects being supplied by the PARTs being connected by the BEAM element. Thus, there will be no mass coupling.

Like the BUSHING, a BEAM element adds 12 variables and equations to an Adams model. The first 6 are displacement values, and the last 6 are force values

A11)

$$\begin{Bmatrix} \Delta_i^J \\ Q_k^J \end{Bmatrix}; i = 1, \cdots 6; k = 7, \cdots 12$$

where

A12)

$$\{\Delta_i^J\} = \begin{Bmatrix} (\vec{\delta} \cdot \vec{J}) \\ (\vec{\theta} \cdot \vec{J}) \end{Bmatrix}$$

A13)

$$\{Q_k^J\} = -[K]\{q_k\} - [C]\{\dot{q}_k\} + \{Qo_k\}; k = 7, \cdots 12$$

The K matrix from the equation above is

$$\begin{bmatrix} k_{11} & 0 & 0 & 0 & 0 & 0 \\ 0 & k_{22} & 0 & 0 & 0 & k_{26} \\ 0 & 0 & k_{33} & 0 & k_{35} & 0 \\ 0 & 0 & 0 & k_{44} & 0 & 0 \\ 0 & 0 & k_{53} & 0 & k_{55} & 0 \\ 0 & k_{62} & 0 & 0 & 0 & k_{66} \end{bmatrix}$$

The damping matrix can be similarly defined.

The *reactions* on the J-MARKER are calculated from

A14)

$$\vec{F}_J = -\vec{F}_i$$

$$\vec{T}_J = -\vec{T}_i - \vec{L} \times \vec{F}_i$$

FIELD

A FIELD provides up to 6 forces and torques between two points (coincident or separated) in the system. Depending on how the user defines it, it can mimic any of the previously-described force elements, except for the action-only SFORCE. Dimensionally similar to the BEAM element, it permits any reasonable, partial or complete definition of the 6 X 6 stiffness and damping matrices. The FIELD has been extensively used in wind turbine analysis to model complex, composite blades inclusive of twist and section property change effects.

NFORCE

The NFORCE creates a *multi-point* force element with linear stiffness and/or damping relationships between up to 351 distinct MARKERS in the Adams model. It has frequently been employed to model FEA-derived attachment compliance and damping to attach model PARTs to otherwise rigid components.

TIRE

The TIRE statement defines several different types of complex tire representations in Adams. Implemented are such tire algorithms as the DELFT, FIALA, and SMITHERS tires, to name a few.

CONTACT

The Adams contact element represents a very powerful method of exploiting the complex geometric shapes of CAD-generated geometry. The elastic properties are specified by a specified stiffness, damping, and force-displacement exponent. In addition, "stiction" and Coulombic friction can be added to the forces. Parasolid-based geometry is the preferred geometry representation. The contacting shapes are non-deforming. When two shapes intersect, a contact volume with centroid, contact normal and tangential vectors is computed. It should be noted that the shapes are permitted to intersect at multiple points.

CONTACT considerations:

1) Stiction should be used with caution. Generally it requires low break-away sliding velocities which can lead to numerical problems with the program integrator.
2) In real-world systems, elastic bodies coming into contact evince two stiffnesses: macro (structural) compliance and micro (Hertzian) compliance. Thus, a contact can be thought of as two springs in a series: a "soft" structural spring, and a "hard" Hertzian spring. The combined stiffnesses will be dominated by the soft spring. This should be taken into account when setting the contact properties. Model units should likewise be taken into account.

3) Contacts should not be used in lieu of constraints to control relative motion. A good example might be the interaction between the bolt and receiver of a hunting rifle. Their interaction could be defined by a contact only, but this would be unwise, as the contact center between any two solids tends to display "jitter" – the wildly changing location of the instantaneous contact centroid. Instead, the interaction of the two solids should be modeled using a cylindrical joint *and* the contact. In doing this, four of the jitter-prone contact force directions are removed from consideration.

4) Contact can be specified between a rigid part and a FLEXBODY, or between two FLEXBODYs. Both of these options will result in a significant increase on model compute time, which may render their use impractical.

Constraint Types

Constraint equations are defined by algebraic variables in the equation set. They are immutable, and their values cannot be changed during an executing analysis. They can, however, be turned on and off between analysis segments using Adams Command File (ACF) commands.

JOINTs

The Adams JOINT element offers useful sets of combined constraints which mimic the behavior of actual connections used in engineering applications. The figure and table below summarize the joints available to the Adams user.

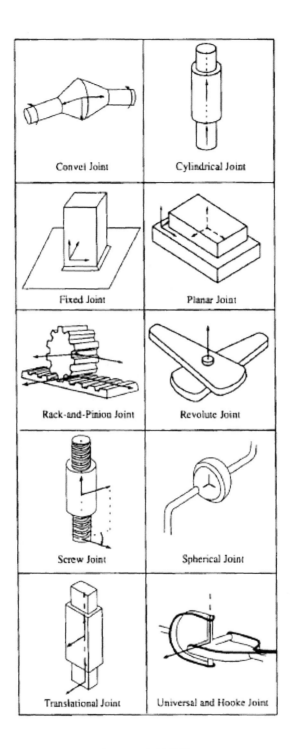

Figure a9 JOINTs

Joint Type	Translational DOFs Removed	Rotational DOFs Removed	Total DOFs Removed	Remarks
CONVEL	3	1	4	Constant velocity joint
CYLINDRICAL	2	2	4	
FIXED	3	3	6	
HOOKE	3	1	4	
PLANAR	1	2	3	
RACKPIN	0.5	0.5	1	Rack & Pinion (Mixed constraint)
REVOLUTE	3	2	5	
SCREW	0.5	0.5	1	Mixed constraint
SPHERICAL	3	0	3	Same as ATPOINT Jprim
TRANSLATIONAL	2	3	5	
UNIVERSAL	3	1	4	

Table A1 – JOINT Types

Some Considerations:

1) The RACKPIN and SCREW joints couple translational motion to translational motion.
2) The reaction force on the I-MARKER PART always acts at the joint I-MARKER while the reaction force on the J-MARKER PART acts at the instantaneous location of the I-MARKER and, thus, its point of application may vary with time.
3) Joints and Jprims can be superimposed.
4) The UNIVERSAL and HOOKE joints function identically, although the HOOKE joint is somewhat easier to implement. When the spin axes of the two PARTs connected by the joint are not parallel, the output shaft spin velocity "wobbles" with respect to the input shaft.
5) The CONVEL joint turns the input and output shafts at the same velocity, regardless of the relative shaft angle.

JPRIMs

The Adams joint primitive – JPRIM – element offers useful sets of combined constraints which mimic the behavior of actual connections used in engineering applications. The figure and table below summarize the jprims available to the Adams user.

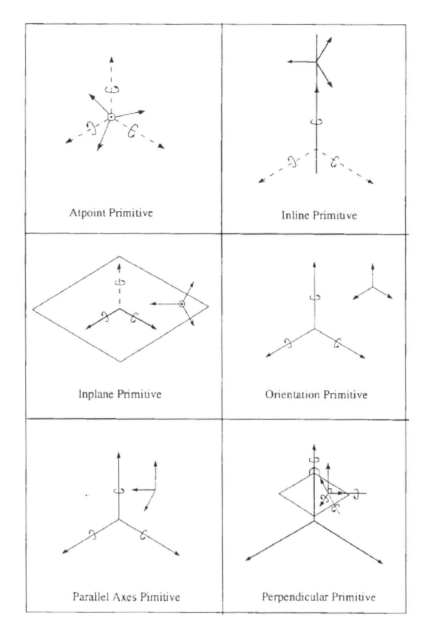

Figure a10 JPRIMs

JprimType	Translational DOFs Removed	Rotational DOFs Removed	Total DOFs Removed	Remarks
ATPOINT	3	0	3	Same as SPHERICAL joint
INLINE	2	0	2	
INPLANE	1	0	1	
ORIENTATION	0	3	3	
PARALELL_AXES	0	2	2	
PERPENDICULAR	0	1	1	

Table A2 – JPRIM Types

Some Considerations:

1) A JPRIM can be thought of as joint pieces. It would be possible to apply the same constraints as a FIXED joint by specifying 3 INPLANE and 3 PERPENDICULAR Jprims between two PARTs, although this would not be a very smart way to do it.

2) The reaction force on the I-MARKER PART always acts at the joint I-MARKER while the reaction force on the J-MARKER PART acts at the instantaneous location of the I-MARKER and, thus, its point of application may vary with time.

GEAR

The GEAR statement defines a gear pair constraint and can be used in conjunction with other constraints to define spur, helical, planetary, bevel, and rack-and-pinion gear pairs. The most important aspect of this constraint is the specification of a constant velocity (CV) MARKER which defines the gear mesh point and motion direction.

COUPLER

The COUPLER relates the translational and/or rotational motion of 2 or 3 joints. While very powerful, it is also complex and specification of the correct coupling ratios can be difficult. A single coupler can capture the related motions of the sun, planetary, and ring gears of a planetary drive. The reader is referred to the Adams HELP utility.

GCONs

The generalized constraint – GCON – represents a recent, and very powerful, addition to the Adams constraint capability. It permits the user to specify virtually any kind of constraint desired. The defining definition is driven to zero during the analysis. This function must be smooth, continuous, and compatible with the other elements of the system. A simple example is given in the 3D pendulum model from the theory section.

User-Defined Elements

In addition to the numerical terms automatically generated when physical components are added to the model, it is possible for the user to add custom defined terms. These take two basic forms: the VARIABLE and the DIFF.

VARIABLE (Algebraic)

The VARIABLE statement defines a custom variable as a scalar algebraic equation. The VARIABLE is also frequently used to simplify the specification of complex functions of already-existing values. This latter application should not be employed frivolously, however, since each VARIABLE employed adds one equation and one state variable to the system equations.

DIFF

The DIFF creates a user-defined state variable in a first-order differential equation. They are frequently used when custom time-integrate quantities are needed. In the excavator model presented in this text, a DIFF is employed to simulate the accretion of dirt in the bucket.

Function Expressions

A host of expressions are available to the user. They are often employed when creating Forces or VARIABLE and DIFF expressions.

Function Type	Use Name	Form	Remarks
Constants	MODE	Integer	Defined by analysis type
	TIME	Scalar	
	PI	Scalar	
	DTOR	Scalar	Degree-to-radian conv
	RTOD	Scalar	Radian-to-degree conv
Displacement	AX,AY,AZ	Scalar	Angular rotation of I about J
	DM,DX,DY,DZ	Scalar	Translational displacements (DM is mag)
	PSI,THETA,PHI	Scalar	Euler Angles (can be discontinuous)
	YAW,PITCH,ROLL	Scalar	Pitch defined + about y axis of J-MARKER (see comment 1 below)
Velocity	VR	Scalar	Radial (line-of-sight) I-J Velocity
	VM,VX,VY,VZ	Scalar	Translational Velocities (VM is mag)
	WM,WX,WY,WZ	Scalar	Angular Velocities (WM is mag) (see comment 1 below)
Acceleration	ACCM,ACCX,ACCY,ACCZ	Scalar	Translational accelerations (ACCM is mag)
	WDTM,WDTX,WDTY,WDTZ	Scalar	Rotational accelerations (WDTM is mag) (see comment 1 below)
Generic Force	FM,FX,FY,FZ	Scalar	MARKER-defined (see comment 2 below)
Generic Torque	TM,TX,TY,TZ	Scalar	MARKER-defined (see comment 2 below)
Element Force or Torque (applied)	BEAM,BUSHING,FIELD, FRICTION,GFORCE, NFORCE,SFORCE, SPDP, VFORCE, VTORQ	Scalar	Name/ID-defined (see comment 3 below)
Element Force or Torque (reaction)	CVCV,JOINT,JPRIM, MOTION,PTCV	Scalar	Name/ID-defined (see comment 3 below)
Arithmetic	IF	Logical	Discontinuous (see comment 4 below)

Interpolation	AKISPL,CUBSPL,CURVE	Scalar	
Mathematical	BISTOP,CHEBY,FORCOS, FORSIN,HAVSIN,IMPACT, POLY,SHF,STEP,STEP5, SWEEP	Scalar	(see comment 4 below)
FORTRAN77	ABS,ACOS,AINT,ANINT, ASIN,ATAN,ATAN2,COS, COSH,EXP,LOG,LOG10, MAX,MIN,MOD,SIGN,SIN, SINH,SQRT,TAN,TANH	Scalar	These functions are identical to those employed by FORTRAN

Table A3 – Function Expressions

Comments:

1) Displacement, velocities, and accelerations all take the same basic form. Using DX as an example, the form is **DX(I,[j],[k])**. This provides the instantaneous scalar value of the I-MARKER origin separation from the J-MARKER origin, measured along the K-MARKER's X-axis. If k is not specified, the separation is measured along the global X-axis. If **j** and **k** are both unspecified, the displacement is the instantaneous scalar value of the I-MARKER origin separation from the global origin, measured along the global X-axis. If DM is called, the K-MARKER must not be specified.

2) Generic requests for the total force acting on a MARKER all take the same basic form. Using FZ as an example, the form is **FZ(I,[j],[k])**. If **k** is omitted, the reference Z-direction defaults to global. If **J** is omitted, only the values applied by ACTIONONLY SFORCEs are captured.

3) In general, a force element can contain up to 6 components. They can be accessed using the form *TYPE(id,jflag,comp,rm)*. The **id** term identifies the element, and **jflag** specifies whether the forces acting on the I-MARKER (**jflag**=0) or on the J-MARKER (**iflag**=1) are desired. For force elements, 8 "slots" are available for the storage of force data. Slots 1 & 5 are reserved for the translational force magnitude and the rotational torque magnitude respectively. Slots 2, 3, & 4 will contain the x-force, y-force, and z-force values, respectively, while slots 6, 7, & 8 will contain the x-torque, y-torque, and z-torque values.

4) The MODE integer variable allows the user to control the analysis flow based on the type of analysis requested. The MODE analysis type key is as follows: 1 → kinematics; 2 → (unused-reserved); 3 → Initial Conditions; 4 → Dynamics; 5 → Statics; 6 → Quasi-statics; 7 → Linear (modal) Analysis.

5) While quite useful in opting between MODE-determined analysis types, the **IF** function is *intrinsically* discontinuous and should never be used in defining time-dependent, numerical function expressions employed in the state equations. Instead, the STEP or STEP5 function should be used, since its definition requires a finite rise time. The STEP function employs a Heavyside cubic polynomial to smoothly change the function value. The STEP5 function employs a faired, quintic approximation to the Heavyside polynomial to change the function value. When employed in displacement-based MOTION constraint functions, the STEP function 2nd derivative terms are discontinuous at zero amplitude, while those of the STEP5 are not.

Special Elements

SENSOR

The SENSOR tracks a user-defined event and initiates a set of simulation controls when the event occurs. When used in conjunction with STEP functions, it proves very useful in dynamically altering the model configuration or in modifying/terminating a program execution.

LSE (Linear State Equation)

An LSE defines the linear relationships between "state transition matrix" (matrix A), "control matrix" (matrix B), the "output matrix" (matrix C), and the "feed forward matrix" (matrix D) of a classical, state-space, (sub-)system representation. Model information resides in Adams MATRIX and ARRAY elements which provide the "bookkeeping" for any necessary matrix operations.

GSE (Generalized State Equation)

The GSE takes the LSE to the next level by permitting non-linear, state-space modeling.

References

1) <u>Introduction to Adams Theory</u>, McConville, J. B. and J. F. McGrath, MDI Feb '99
2) <u>V68 User's Guide MSC/MSC Nastran Basic Dynamic Analysis)</u>, Blakely, Ken, MSC, '93
3) <u>Mechanische Systeme</u>, Hiller, M., Springer-Verlag, Berlin, 1983
4) <u>Fundamentals of Vehicle Dynamics</u>, Gillespie, T. D., Society of Automotive Engineers, Inc., ISBN 1-56091-199-9
5) <u>NODE-ANALOGOUS, SPARSITY-ORIENTED METHODS FOR SIMULATION OF MECHANICAL DYNAMIC SYSTEMS</u>, (Orlandea, N.) University Microfilms, A XEROX Company, Ann Arbor, Michigan 74-15,821
6) <u>The dynamic Simulation of a Moving Vehicle Subject to Transient Steering Inputs Using the Adams Computer Program</u>, McConville, J. B. and J. C. Angell, ASME Paper 84-DET-2
7) <u>The Combination of Mechanical System Simulation and Finite Element Analysis Software to Model Structural Failure in an Aircraft Accident Investigation</u>, Savoni, G. (Boeing, Long Beach CA), McConville, J (MDI Ann Arbor MI), Proceedings of the MSC Nastran Conference, Long Beach CA, 1999.